Mike,

At this  just want to tell you how much I appreciate your _friendship_. It is a gift that I shall always treasure. Thank you for your understanding and sensitivity to the needs of others around you. Thank you for the guidance and advice you have offered to me _personally_ and as an Officer.

I hope you, in some small way, find this book helpful in your endeavor as a police Officer. I hope that you too shall continue to be one of the "good cops."

May the Lord bless you richly in all of your life, goals, and ambitions.

With deepest appreciation
I am

Officer Bettye Spivey
December 13, 1977

Good Cops/Bad Cops

Good Cops/Bad Cops

Memoirs of a Police Psychiatrist

Edward E. Shev, M. D.
and Jeremy Joan Hewes

SAN FRANCISCO BOOK COMPANY, INC.
San Francisco 1977

Library of Congress Cataloging in Publication Data

Shev, Edward E.
    Good cops, bad cops.

    Bibliography.
    Includes index.
    1. Shev, Edward E. 2. Police psychiatrists—United States—Biography. I. Hewes, Jeremy Joan, joint author. II. Title.
HV7936.P75S483   362.8   77-10
ISBN 0-913374-69-5

Printed in the United States of America
10 9 8 7 6 5 4 3 2 1

To my wife ELEANOR *and my daughter* ANNE

". . . this savage in the service of civilization—this strange composite of the Roman and Spartan, the monk and the corporal, this spy incapable of falsehood, this virgin detective. . ."

VICTOR HUGO
(description of Inspector Javert in *Les Miserables*)

Contents

Foreword

I FIRST began working with Dr. Shev in 1968, shortly after he had established and fine-tuned the components of a psychiatric in-service program for police in Sausalito, California. As Chief of Police in the nearby town of Novato, I asked Dr. Shev to help evaluate candidates for recruitment and promotion, and to direct the free-wheeling, give-and-take group sessions with police officers that had proved so successful in Sausalito. Later, when I moved on to become Chief of Police in St. Louis County and Boston, I repeatedly sought Dr. Shev's help in implementing various phases of this psychiatric program, and I found that the benefits to each officer, as well as to each department, were astonishing.

This book will undoubtedly create extensive controversy in the police field, but I hope that police officials will not react to it in overprotective, secretive, or defensive ways. We in police work need to stop hiding our weaknesses and bring our problems out in front. We need to talk about personnel problems, the inherent stresses of police work, the lack of proper selection, the lack of proper supervision, the lack of proper administration. If we do not, perhaps this book will cause officials and citizens alike to demand from their police departments the kind of accountability Dr. Shev calls for here.

One of the major problems that has rarely, if ever, been discussed—and which Dr. Shev brings out here—is the fact that police recruitment officials are not selecting the best possible candidates for police work. He states that approximately 35 per cent of all police are psychologically unsuited for police work and should never have been hired. I agree with this figure as far as police in California are concerned, but from my experience in other areas of the country, I must regretfully conclude that this percentage may be even higher, especially in large urban police departments, and even in rural departments in certain areas of the country. Moreover—and, again, Dr. Shev covers this point well—the officers who were hired incorrectly to begin with have been left to their own devices for too long. When weaknesses have inevitably developed, these problem officers have not been assisted by the administrations of their own departments.

There are many doubting Thomases in the police field, and many citizens as well, who may take exception to the idea that their police need psychiatric help. Their assumption is that there must be something "wrong" with police that psychiatrists must come in and "fix." Dr. Shev's premise, however, is that even for the many good cops in the field today, the pressures of police work are so extraordinary that *no one* can be expected to cope with them without guidance from a professional psychiatrist. I heartily concur—in fact, there are many instances where the Chief and his department are both dependent on the counsel of a police psychiatrist.

In St. Louis, for example, a psychiatrist evaluated prospective juvenile aide personnel and found that one officer had a personality trait that would definitely have created difficulties in his dealing with young males. In the department's helicopter patrol program, an officer who had extensive helicopter combat experience was being considered for a chief supervisory role. But the psychiatric evaluation revealed that the officer was actually afraid of heights, apparently as a result of numerous combat missions in Vietnam.

Needless to say, if either man had been hired, everyone connected with either program would have suffered, as would the effectiveness of the entire department. No other tests, no bureaucratic application forms, no battery of psychological screening devices could have given us the information that one psychiatrist detected in one interview with each of these candidates.

In the case of entry-level candidates in the department, many were turned down after evaluation by this psychiatrist. Nevertheless, seven of those who had been rejected were later hired by police departments in neighboring areas. All seven candidates failed to complete their probationary period with those departments—each for reasons that had been apparent to the psychiatrist in the first interview.

Dr. Shev calls it the "psychotherapeutic interview," and it works. I recall one occasion in Novato when he spoke for one hour with each of four candidates for promotion. I had worked with these men for more than seven years. Dr. Shev's perceptions of these officers provided insights into their characters that I had intuited but had never articulated, even after so many years of close association.

In Boston I found that the usual police problems were further compounded by an archaic statewide civil service system, a departmental hierarchy that never concerned itself with the personnel, a department where supervision was totally unknown, and an archaic, suicidal shift program where officers doubled back within eight hours to do a second tour of duty in one day. This was the condition of the

3

police when the busing crisis erupted in Boston in 1974 which weakened the department even further. Although psychiatrists have still not been used in many key areas, some progress has been made. Numerous alcoholic and other emotional problems pervaded the Boston Police Department to the extent that it was necessary to begin a stress program where non-drinking alcoholic police officers were assigned to counsel, with the aid of a staff psychologist, officers in the department who had emotional problems. But real improvement will not be possible—in Boston and in so many other departments—until psychiatrists are utilized in all phases of selection, promotion, and in-service counseling.

The people who work in the police field must be carefully chosen, must be well supervised, and must be given every assistance possible to help them perform their difficult tasks. Police work is too important and the work is too full of unseen pressures for our society to neglect the personnel we employ to enforce our laws. Dr. Shev and the too few other psychiatrists working in the police field are filling a tremendous void by developing a psychiatric in-service program that every department in the United States should undertake. I beg citizens, appointed officials, and elected politicians in all jurisdictions of this country to read the experiences and the recommendations that Dr. Shev has included in this book. I ask every reader to consider whether we can wait much longer to implement this program wherever police departments exist.

ROBERT J. DI GRAZIA
Director of Police
Montgomery County, Maryland

Preface

THE FIRST PART of this book is a chronological account of my work with members of the police department and city council of Sausalito, California. Where necessary, I have changed some names to protect the privacy of individuals. Dialogue has been reconstructed faithfully from memory and notes; while it is not verbatim, it does retain the substance of actual conversations that took place.

I am very grateful for the continued assistance and support of Charles Brown, Ed Kreins, and the many chiefs of police in California with whom I have worked—notably, James Wright of Sausalito, Al Klemme of Novato, Larry Higgins of Petaluma, and Ken Harns of Pleasant Hill. My deep appreciation to Colonel George Halverson, John Longstreth, and Colonel John Plants of the Michigan State Police; Robert Wasserman, Director of the Police Academy, Boston; Thomas Cahill, former Chief of Police of San Francisco; Charles Gain, present Chief of Police of San Francisco. For their help in the early stages of this project, I am indebted to Donald Stokes and Julie Manson, as well as to my secretary,

5

Kathleen McFadden, and transcriber, Marjean McClure. Many thanks, too, to the hundreds of people in various police departments throughout the country whose help and support has been invaluable.

EDWARD E. SHEV, M.D.

San Francisco
February 1977

I WISH TO EXPRESS my fond thanks to Pat Murphy McClelland, Jane Vandenburgh, and Don McClelland for their help at an essential point in the preparation of this manuscript, to Elena Perkins for timely information, and to Patricia Holt for editorial guidance and endless patience.

JEREMY JOAN HEWES

San Francisco
February 1977

An Interview

The following is a composite of remarks and comments made by police officers over a twelve-year period. It is not typical of most cops' response to a psychiatric in-service program, but it does bring out some of the more significant issues that a police psychiatrist must confront in any police department in the country.

Cop: Dr. Shev, I asked to see you in private because I've had enough of your so-called psychiatric program and I think you should hear somebody from the department tell you how lousy it is.

Shev: Well, all right. But why haven't you brought it up in the group sessions with the other men?

Cop: Because the discussion would just bog down to a lot of shouting and they'd accuse me of a personality clash or something like that. You said we could make private appointments with you to discuss personal gripes and that's what I'm doing.

Shev: Do you think maybe it *is* a personality clash?

Cop: No, I don't think so, and anyway it doesn't matter. The things I want to get off my chest don't have anything to do with you as a person, but they do have a lot to do with the program and what it's doing to cops like me.

Shev: Okay. Go ahead.

Cop: First of all, I think you invade a person's privacy when you ask about his background and his family and his feelings about his mother and father, and all. That is just nobody's business and I don't see that it has anything to do with whether I can do my duty as a police officer or not.

Shev: You mean the interview I gave to you when you first applied to the department? After you passed the background check?

Cop: Yes.

Shev: Did it enrage you at the time?

Cop: No, I was just trying to get through it, but later—especially after the group sessions when you got into things like racial prejudice and homosexuality and impotence—I thought to myself, "My god! This is just too much!"

Shev: Wait a minute, now, let's take this one step at a time. You think that the interviews I give to new applicants are an invasion of privacy. First of all, you don't have to participate in the interview, you know.

Cop: Yeah, but then you'd recommend against my getting hired.

Shev: Yes, I would. But do you know why?

Cop: Because you wouldn't have any control over me after that. You would never know if I hated my father, which I guess is the standard you use to figure out if I'd make a bad cop.

Shev: Why do you think I want to have control over you? I don't, you know, after you're hired. I'm not even the one who decides *if* you get hired. All I'm here for is to offer counseling services, direct the group sessions, and give lectures on issues you confront in police work. Even if I wanted to, there is just no way that I could hold the information you gave me in the first interview over your head.

Cop: But why do you want that information in the first place? What does any of it have to do with whether I can make a burglary investigation or arrest a drunk driver?

Shev: A lot. Maybe you missed my lecture on the kinds of influences that affect us as we grow up, or maybe you weren't listening—so you don't know how really crucial all this is. Am I right in my recollection that your father was an alcoholic?

Cop: Yes, but if you think that's going to make me beat up every drunk in town—.

Shev: No, it's not that simple at all, but don't you think this community has a right to explore with you your feelings about drunks before we put a gun and a badge on you and send you out to arrest drunks?

Cop: Well, okay, I see your point there, but you go deeper than that, you want to know if I *loved* my father, *and* my mother, *and* my sister—.

Shev: (grinning)—and your uncles and your cousins and the butcher down the block?

Cop: (grinning) Yeah.

Shev: All right, now let me try something: if you were to ask a dozen people why cops get into police work in the first place, what do you think they'd say?

Cop: I don't know. I don't think it would be all that positive.

Shev: Well, many of them would say that cops are authoritarian types who like to use the uniform and the gun to strut around showing their authority and make people buckle under. Do you agree with that?

Cop: Hell, no. I can't speak for anybody else, but I got into it because I wanted to help people, I wanted to be of service to the community. You do far more work helping people to solve everyday problems than you ever do knocking heads around.

Shev: Right. And as it happens, you do speak for many of your peers, because most cops come into police work with the notion that they *will* help people, that they'll be a part of a service profession. In fact, I find the motivating impulse is very much like a doctor or minister or social worker—it's the service idea that attracts them, not the power or the salary or the uniform or anything else.

Cop: Well, I think that's good.

Shev: It is to a degree. Some cops think that the only way they can help society is to punish wrongdoers—they'll take a guy who's broken the law and push him around, just to "give him a lesson he'll never forget," that sort of thing.

Cop: That's illegal and it's immoral. I know some cops do it, but I never will.

Shev: Why not?

Cop: Well, it's taking the law into your own hands, for one thing. We can't be the judge and jury in these situations. Besides, if I start teaching "lessons" like that to people on my beat I'll never be trusted there again.

Shev: Right. And have you ever run across the kind of guy who tries to curb that impulse to be rough with the people he's arresting?

Cop: You mean he gets mad and tries to hold it back?

Shev: Yes.

Cop: Sure, a lot of cops feel that way, I do too sometimes. But you just have to learn to hold it back.

Shev: Okay. Some cops are better equipped to cope with it than others, right?

Cop: Right.

Shev: But suppose I told you that more than one-third of all cops on the street today are psychologically ill-equipped to handle the pressures of police work? I mean these are cops who never should have been hired in the first place—they are a danger to society.

Cop: One-third of *all* cops? I don't believe it.

Shev: Take a look around you. We've reduced the number of bad cops in our department, but the problem is still very much apparent in most cities. The thing is, you can't spot a bad cop with psychological screening tests, you have to have a trained psychiatrist interview him, not only about police work but about his background, his feelings about his family, his frustrations, aspirations, and so forth. You come to my lecture on the triangle of life and the rescue fantasy theory and you'll see why this is all so important.

Cop: All right, but why do you turn these lectures into discussions of the sins of the world? We *know* about racism and pornography—.

Shev: Do you?

Cop: Well, I mean we know enough to enforce the law, that's what we're there for, isn't it? Not to be two-bit shrinks but to bust a porno house if that's the chief's orders, or to arrest a law-breaker no matter what his color if he really did break the law.

Shev: All right, let's discuss this issue of racism, which you must agree is a very sensitive subject.

Cop: Of course I do.

Shev: Let me tell you as a professional psychiatrist that everybody in this country has some kind of prejudice in his head—we may not know it, but we do—and cops are no exception. What I'm trying to do is to get you guys to talk about it, open up and confront feelings you may not know exist, so that when you work with minorities on the street you'll be aware of personal hangups that may stand in the way of professional conduct. You know that 55 to 60 per cent of all street crimes are committed by minorities? Well, some cops *unconsciously* assume that all minorities are suspect. I've known a lot of cops who will rough up a black person because deep down they hate all blacks.

Cop: Okay, I can see that. But you always go so much deeper into these things. The other day you not only talked to us about pornography, you went into the entire history of pornography and showed us pornographic slides to boot! I mean to tell you, Doctor, it embarrassed the hell out of me.

Shev: Did it make you mad?

Cop: Yes!

Shev: I mean, did my showing the slides make you mad or did just the idea of pornographic pictures make you mad?

Cop: Well, both. I *hate* pornography.

Shev: All right. That is your right as a human being. But it is not your right as a cop. Do you realize what could happen if you participated in a bust on an adult bookstore and you walked in and saw all those pictures on the wall and on the shelves? If you hadn't thought of it before, if you hadn't confronted the fact that this stuff makes you blind with rage, you might very well get mad and lose control. One step out of line from you and the whole department could look silly—not to mention charges that the cops got rough and lost their heads.

Cop: But that's part of the job. You talk to us about things that have nothing to do with police work—impotence, for example—and you have sessions with our wives and talk about our sex lives and all of that. I still don't know what value these sessions have, and I still think you're invading my privacy when you have them.

Shev: Well, remember that I can't invade your privacy unless you volunteer information that brings me into your private life—and then it's not an "invasion" because you've given me the information in the first place, right?

Cop: Yes, but I wouldn't tell you about these things unless you asked me to tell you.

Shev: But that's the whole point—that's why I *do* ask you, don't you see?

Cop: No.

Shev: All right, look: it's not as if every once in a while a cop has a bad day: a lot of the time *all* his days are bad days.

People yell at him, try to bribe him, abuse his uniform, involve him in ugly brawls and on and on it goes—you know this line better than I do.

Cop: We all know it, but that's our job.

Shev: No, wait. Hear me out. Unless a cop knows how to cope with all these pressures he's going to start taking it personally or get mad or let it all build up inside him. Then he comes home and takes it out on the wife and kids. They get mad back—the wife especially, because she has her own problems to contend with—and I mean there could be a big shouting match or there could just be a kind of silent intolerance of each other. Obviously it's going to hurt their sex life, and that's going to add to his troubles, and the next day you know what happens—.

Cop: He takes it back on the street with him.

Shev: Yes. He's got a very short fuse, and he may blow up at the slightest provocation. Or he may just hold it all in and let it eat away at him. The outcome is that he loses all sense of being in a service profession, and he starts getting negative. Violations make him madder and he finds himself overreacting much of the time, letting his emotions get in the way. Now he's become the worst kind of police officer there is: a *punitive cop.* The people on the street sense this and react negatively to him, which makes him more angry. Then when he goes home he's not even fit to live with. So now his professional life and his home life are shot to hell, and the point is, he doesn't know what to *do* about it.

Cop: I just think that's so rare—

Shev: Is it? No, it's just the opposite: it's much more common than people realize. You thought that discussion on impotence was wrong, but do you remember who did most of the talking? It was your fellow officers. I actually said very little.

Cop: Yeah, but what you did say was stuff none of us knew about.

Shev: Well, that's what I'm here for, after all. But listen, if what I say offends you or makes you embarrassed in any way, why don't you bring it out at the group session? You may break the ice for others who've been holding back the same thing.

Cop: Well, yes, I think I will.

Part I

1

A Shrink to Screen Recruits

My work with police began rather casually. While emptying my garbage one evening early in 1965, I met my neighbor Charles Brown, who was city manager of our town of Sausalito, California.

"I was just thinking about you, Ed," Brown called as he climbed the steep, narrow street toward my carport. "I'd like to get your reaction to a new plan for avoiding another mess in the police department."

I was familiar with that "mess." It had culminated with Brown's firing of the police chief about a year before, amid charges of corruption and incompetence in the department. Several other police officers had resigned or been removed after the chief's termination, and the controversy still had not died down.

Brown had dismissed the chief for poor administration and training of his department, but an undercurrent of suspicion among residents had contributed to the crisis. The level of crime was far too high for a city of 6,000—$500,000 in robberies in one year alone—and local newspapers reported charges of officers' drinking on the job or taking payoffs for giving "extra" protection to businesses. Some citizens claimed that the police themselves were burglars; when a resident notified police that he would be away, the cops would promise to watch the home and then loot it themselves without fear of detection. There was even talk that one policeman used his job to indulge a personal aberration—as a peeping tom.

Nor was the city council above suspicion at the time. The police chief had contested his removal, and hearings before a citizens' board of appeal revealed that the council had hired this man even though he had not made a passing score on the written exam for chief. In fact, no one in the Sausalito department had made the required 70 per cent on the standard police officers' test. So public sentiment toward the city's police and government was at low ebb.

"I'm optimistic about the situation now," Brown continued. "We have a chief who's from outside the department, and he seems to be taking charge very well. He's even convinced the council to add five new officers to the twelve we have at present—and I have trouble getting money for light bulbs! But the new policy I wanted to discuss with you was suggested by a group of residents. They wanted to have psychological screening of the applicants for police jobs. What do you think of the idea, Ed?"

I knew about the proposal and had heard that a psychoanalyst who lived in Sausalito had already begun interviewing applicants. "That notion has been raised in the psychiatric literature and it's a good one," I said, "but I don't know of any cities that have had long-term experience with such a program. You have someone doing screening now, don't you, Charlie?"

"We did for a few weeks," the city manager answered, "but he's going abroad and has resigned from the job. That's why I wanted to talk to you about the idea. I'd like to propose your name to the council as his replacement."

Screening potential cops was definitely a good idea, and it appealed to me. Yet I wasn't sure that my full schedule would accommodate another project. I asked Brown to let me think about it for a day, and when I got back in the house I glanced at my calendar for that month. It indicated that I already had plenty to do—in addition to a full-time psychiatric and neurologic practice, there were several evening meetings of hospital committees, a fund-raising event for visually handicapped persons, a meeting to plan for maintaining open space in Sausalito, and a weekend neurological conference in southern California. Still, the prospect of helping select better police intrigued me, and I traced back over my own attitude toward cops.

My first impressions about police came from my parents. They had immigrated to Nebraska from Russia early in this century to escape czarist rule. I remember hearing the story of my father's experience with Russian police when I was about six. My uncle, who had also fled Russia, had come to visit, and we had just finished an hour-long Sunday dinner. The two men had talked about their homeland throughout the meal; then my father looked troubled and when he spoke his voice sounded angry. It was the first time my brothers and I had heard him talk this way.

"For two years I had been the master of my blacksmith shop in Kiev. Then one day, almost at sunset, three policemen came to the shop and told me to put out the fire—I was a 'conscript' and would be serving the army from now on. They let me return home that night, but one of the police waited outside my house so that I would not escape.

"In the morning I was taken to a small railroad station outside the city and put aboard a train that was crowded with other conscripts. After two days of traveling with little food and no sleep, we arrived at a mining camp in the Ural Mountains. I was to be blacksmith for the mining operation, making tools and repairing cars and tracks. That camp was my 'home' for three years.

"I had not done anything wrong," he continued, his voice sounding even more enraged. "I was taken because I was young and strong and good at my craft. The police just picked me out and took my life away from me. That I will never forget, and that is why I planned and worked for many years to get away from the czar and his police state. In Nebraska I have my life back again."

I heard such stories many times as a child, and I felt both fear and awe that police could have such power. Yet whenever my father told his story, he ended by saying that the U.S. Constitution had given him back his life. His reverence for American freedoms was as strong as his hatred of the Russian oppression, and this attitude permeated our lives. Thus, I grew up with a respect for a government of laws and individual rights, but with the knowledge that both could be abused by the misdirected power of police.

As I recalled my father's experience, some of my own apprehensions about police came back, too—the mixture of fear and respect that most people probably feel toward cops. Somehow we're always at our most vulnerable when dealing with police, whether it's asking for help, feeling embarrassed or indignant about a traffic violation, or resenting the authority of someone with a gun and a badge.

And I thought of my reaction when the storm erupted in the Sausalito Police Department in late 1963. I had been concerned for the safety of my family and home, and my uneasiness had increased as rumors and charges about corruption became a principal topic of conversation among residents. Like many of my neighbors, I was angry and frustrated with city officials for allowing such poor selection and administration of the police.

That night, thinking about Brown's suggestion, I realized that all my concerns boiled down to one basic concern: police are the only people society allows to carry and use guns to enforce law and maintain order at their discretion;

thus they should be the healthiest, most stable members of society. Yet the upheaval in the Sausalito department showed that this was not the standard for choosing cops. In fact, the real problem with police selection was that no standards at all were used.

I was to find out later that in virtually every city, town, county, or state, police traditionally have been hired on a helter-skelter basis. Perhaps they had a cousin in the department, scored well on a civil service exam, or made a good impression on the chief. In many instances they were men who did not or could not qualify for any other work. Few, if any, methods existed for evaluating the emotional status or personality traits that might affect police in their work. In short, we were arming people we knew almost nothing about—and giving them license to kill if they saw fit.

Today many communities still hire police without adequately screening, training, or counseling them. Time and time again in recent years the headlines have reported graft and corruption within police departments or the arrest or even shooting of the wrong persons by police. To me, as I consider the vagaries that still exist in the selection of cops, these reports are no surprise.

The screening program for police was particularly important for Sausalito, because it was instituted during the social turmoil of the mid-1960s. An old fishing village at the foot of the hills along San Francisco Bay just north of the Golden Gate, this small city had become a gathering place for a variety of social elements. On any weekend the sidewalks of the central district were crowded with as many as 50,000 tourists and "street people," including people on hard drugs and runaway youngsters who spilled over from San Francisco's soon-to-be-famous Haight-Ashbury district. These numbers alone posed problems for the dozen-man police department, and hostilities developed between young people and local merchants that some officers were not equipped to handle. The men had been trained in standard police procedure and knew the local statutes, but many of them had great difficulty keeping cool when faced with a group of taunting, hostile kids on one side and, on the other, an angry shopkeeper demanding that the streets be cleared of "this rabble." In such a situation a policeman must use discretion and treat both sides with friendly objectivity—a tall order for the best of cops and a near impossibility for those whose personal problems distort their judgment.

At that time, too, racial tensions were reaching a peak in Sausalito. The disparity between the primarily white affluent residential areas and the largely black housing developments of neighboring Marin City had grown increasingly intense, and a vicious circle of misunderstanding and reaction between blacks and whites was escalating. A focal point for this stress was the school board's plan to integrate the district's four elementary schools, which meant that many Marin City and Sausalito children would be bused out of their neighborhoods.

Thus, Sausalito could not afford to have a corrupt or ineffective police force, nor could the city have cops whose individual problems and attitudes might increase hostilities or make tense situations explode. The change in police chiefs and election of a reform-minded council had improved the prospects for avoiding trouble within the department, and I felt that this new screening program promised still more improvement. So I decided to take on the job.

The day after our conversation I phoned Charles Brown to tell him of my decision. But I also confided my misgivings about whether police and city officials were truly prepared to have a "shrink" in their midst. The principal source of my uneasiness was the uproar following a somewhat similar program in San Francisco several years previously. The police chief at that time had authorized a trial program of psychological testing for police recruits. The psychologist who administered and evaluated the tests reported to the chief that 90 per cent of the applicants tested were not psychologically fit for police work. These studies revealed police recruits who were described as "paranoid," or "sadistic," or "unstable," or "depressed."

When these findings were reported within the department, the police association, civil service officials, and senior officers all protested bitterly. No one with any authority for hiring police wanted to share it with a psychologist or psychiatrist, nor did anyone associated with the department want it known that the tests had cast serious doubt on the suitability of young police officers. The pressure to squelch the test results and to discontinue the program was tremendous, and the San Francisco chief ultimately yielded to it.

I wasn't in on this experiment, but in a sense I had been burned by it. The San Francisco program had been killed before it could even get off the ground, and here I was proposing to tell Sausalito what cops to hire or reject. I didn't relish the reception I knew I'd get from many police, who would regard any shrink and any screening process with suspicion or even hostility. In my twenty years of practice I'd learned firsthand that people often joke about, tease, or malign psychiatrists openly. This is simply a fact of life in my profession—but I've never been unaffected by it. In fact, that sense of frustration over the suspicion and hostility directed at me, not for any personal reason but because of my job, is one very basic thing I have in common with most cops.

"I think our situation is quite different from San Francisco's," Brown responded to my account of that short-lived experiment. "For one thing, our council approved this program before it started, and the idea came from a citizens' group. That ought to take some of the political pressure off. Besides, the new chief is completely in favor of screening, and because he didn't come from the ranks of our department, he's not likely to cave in to pressure from other cops or outraged citizens."

"You're right, Charlie. But I did want you to know the sort of reaction we might get from some people."

"Aw, we can weather it," the city manager said; then he paused, as if waiting for me to disagree. But I wasn't giving him an argument, so he continued. "Okay, the council's approval of your nomination is just a formality, and they should take care of that on Saturday. I'll call you next week and we'll get together with Chief Huck so you can begin screening."

The meeting with Brown and the new chief, Kenneth Huck, took place as promised, and after talking with Huck I was very encouraged about working with his department. He was an informal, very approachable man, the sort of leader who has the respect of his officers while enjoying a good rapport with them. And Huck showed a firm commitment to the screening program, which meant that I wouldn't be out on a limb somewhere, working blind. (It also meant that I wouldn't have to take the flack alone, if and when it came.)

The first call for a screening interview came just a few days after my meeting with the chief. We had agreed that each candidate must come to my office for the interview, as this would both establish my role as medical professional and make clear to the applicant that our meeting was confidential. And it took the candidate away from the more secure territory of his usual environment, so he did not have a familiar role or set of props to camouflage his personality.

The first few interviews went smoothly. I had no difficulty evaluating these men by the standard for a basically "normal" individual—someone who has the usual amount of fears and anxiety but is stable enough not to overreact in a situation of stress. And Chief Huck concurred with my recommendation for each applicant.

Yet I felt that something was missing. Certainly the

screening had begun to serve its purpose by weeding out candidates who would make bad cops, but it offered no basis for determining who would make good cops. So I went to the University of California library at Berkeley to study the literature on police and psychological aspects of their work. But the published studies did me no good at all. They tended to isolate the emotional problems of police without answering any of my questions about what makes a good cop: what are the basic functions of police work, and what emotional burdens do these functions impose? What sort of person goes into police work? Does it take something other than a "normal" individual to be a good cop? I came away from this research with confirmation of some negative stereotypes about police—the "paranoid, hostile authority figure"—but with few positive findings.

Realizing that the information about police I needed had not yet been gathered, I decided to go to the source—the men themselves. If I could interview police who were good at their jobs and watch them in action, I'd be able to identify the characteristics that make a good cop. And I would add a new and much needed dimension to the psychiatric screening process.

I phoned Tom Cahill, with whom I had worked as a consultant and who was then chief of the San Francisco force, and outlined my thinking to him. Because any psychiatric probing of police was a touchy subject in his department, it was understood that this research would be done discreetly. But since I had made some psychiatric studies of the police files on pornography, I was familiar to many of the men and had a topic of common interest to get the conversation started.

The chief gave me the names of fifty men he considered good cops, and over a period of several weeks I met with these men in their offices or squad rooms, or talked informally with them before or after they went on duty. I did not attempt to speak with women officers because I knew I would not be working with female police in Sausalito. Because these sessions were both sensitive and informal, I did not use notes or a tape recorder. But my experience in interviewing and assessing personalities allowed me to retain much of the specific information from these discussions and to form an over all picture of the behavior of a good policeman.

The first characteristic of these men was that they all were primarily interested in helping people. A typical response to my question of why they went into police work would be: "Oh, it's sort of a kick, you know? There isn't a day that's the same; there's not a day that I'm not asked to perform some kind of service that I think is absolutely crazy, but I do it because it's my job and it makes people happy." Another officer might add: "And I get a great boost out of being able to use my investigative skills to follow a case through to its conclusion—but the main thing is that I help people when they're in trouble."

Another distinction was that these men didn't take their work home with them. They were able to derive satisfaction from helping people in their work—or to put aside the frustrations of not always being able to help—and also find fulfillment in their family life and outside interests. Most of the fifty men I interviewed were married and had children, and they stated that when their work was particularly taxing, they could be refreshed and renewed by spending time with their wives and kids—perhaps coping with family problems, but participating fully in the normal flow of life that their jobs at times obscured. Then they would be ready to return to work with a balanced perspective.

These interviews also revealed some surprising facts about how little physical force these men used in their jobs. For instance, the fifty officers had drawn their guns an average of only one and a half times in ten years of service, and few had ever used their nightsticks. Instead, their approach was one of empathy and understanding—they would send a drunk home in a taxi rather than arrest him; they didn't rough up people when they arrested them, nor did they get overly concerned about the fact that pornographic films and books were available in certain areas of the city.

A profile of the personality that makes an ideal policeman began to emerge. Because of the rather roundabout nature of my interviews, I did not have exhaustive personal information about each man, but I had learned enough about their backgrounds to draw some general conclusions. These men were intelligent, with IQ's between 110 and 140, but few of them had any college training. They were dedicated to the department; in fact, it seemed to represent a parental figure to them. And while they exhibited a moderate amount of suspicion or paranoia, this was well controlled and did not impede their "soft" approach to handling problems with citizens.

But my most unexpected finding was that more than half of the men came from broken homes. In some cases, the parents were divorced or separated and the child had only one person to relate to as both mother and father. In other instances the home was what psychiatric jargon labels "occultly" broken—both parents lived at home but one was ill or alcoholic or so passive that he or she did not participate in a normal parental relationship. (The "absent" parent in most of these men's background was the father.) This finding especially fascinated me, because the men had somehow overcome difficult childhood experiences of a broken home and resolved their own personal conflicts and feelings to become effective police officers.

Now I had some raw data about good cops. Although my fifty interviews could not be considered significant in statistical terms, they offered definite clues to the type of person who was effective in police work. And this correlation between a personality type and a certain job tallied with an earlier experience I'd had as neurological consultant to an airline. In working with the corporation's medical director and personnel staff to establish psychological testing for hiring of stewardesses, I found that a "normal," middle-of-the-road person did not make the best cabin attendant. Rather, the type of woman most suited to becoming a stewardess was one who had a tendency toward a slight depression which was relieved by her satisfaction from the constant service the job entails. Thus, she *liked* to work hard and—because of the personality trait of tendency toward depression—was highly motivated to do her job well.

Perhaps—as in the stewardess's job—some particular trait or need also could make a person a good cop. I felt that I was coming close to the answer to one of my early questions about police: was a "normal" person necessarily material for a good cop, or did this specialized and demanding job require something more? I wasn't sure, but at least I had this sketchy profile of a good cop to add to my consideration as I interviewed and evaluated potential police.

2
The First Candidates

So I RESUMED the interviews for Sausalito, armed with the findings of my new research. I felt more confident now, and as I talked with each candidate I found points of comparison with my profile of a good cop.

One day's interviews were particularly revealing. I met with three men, all competing for one patrolman's job. They had similar backgrounds—all had some preliminary training in police work, came from small cities or suburbs, and had gone beyond high school in their educations. Their interviews with me were typical of the types of men who reach this final stage of the application process and of the topics I generally discuss with candidates. (In fact, those interviews might have taken place last month, instead of more than ten years ago.) Yet the men themselves were quite different. Excerpts from these three interviews show both the similarities of these men's aspirations and the important differences among them.

I'm talking with John Thomas Campbell, twenty years old, who was referred for psychiatric interview for the position of patrolman. Mr. Campbell is aware that this interview is being taped. He understands that I don't make final decisions and that my evaluation is just one part of his selection process.

If you have any questions about this, please take them to the chief, not to me. Okay?

Campbell: Yes.

You've been working in the department how long?

Campbell: Eight months.

Why are you interested in police work?

Campbell: Well, I got interested in it because I knew a policeman, and he explained to me that every day was different, and just the matter of the same routine didn't appeal to me at all. So I started investigating police work and found out that I liked it.

What do you like about it?

Campbell: I like the non-routine, first of all. I think it's good pay for the work you do. I get some satisfaction out of knowing that I've helped the general population—it doesn't have to be one person—in some minor thing that I do.

Like what?

Campbell: Well, right now I'm a cadet there [a cadet handles office duties and observes officers], but I feel like I'm helping people when they come in to the front office with accident reports and that type of thing. And it gives me a good feeling.

How do you feel about wearing a uniform?

Campbell: That doesn't bother me—I'm proud of it. I think it's symbolic of police work. It really doesn't bother me, if that's what you mean.

I didn't mean anything.

Campbell: But I enjoy it. I think I look good in the uniform.

Where were you born?

Campbell: Vallejo, California.

How far have you gone in school?

Campbell: I've got fifty-six units toward my Associate of Arts degree in Administration of Justice.

Are your parents still alive?

Campbell: No—my father passed away in February.

What was the cause; how old was he?

Campbell: He had a heart attack—he was forty-seven.

What kind of heart attack?

Campbell: I don't know. He had three attacks before then. The first one was in 1962.

So you were about sixteen when he had the first one?

Campbell: Yes, I was a sophomore in high school.

Were you scared at the time?

Campbell: Very. I was at home when he had it. We were having dinner, and he got up from the table to get some more food from the kitchen. He had complained of chest pains earlier in the day—he thought it was gas or something. He got up, then he fell to the floor; he couldn't breathe, and his lips started turning purple—same with his fingernails.

What did you do?

Campbell: I loosened his belt and called for the fire department while my mother was trying to make sure he could breathe okay. The fire department applied oxygen and took him to the hospital. He took three months to recover from that attack.

What kind of person was your father?

Campbell: He was a strict, no-nonsense person—he didn't take any nonsense.

Pretty strict with you?

Campbell: Well, now that I look back, he wasn't as strict as he should've been, but at the time I thought he was. He made sure I realized the consequences of everything before I started.

What do you mean?

Campbell: There came times when I wanted to get out on

my own, to get a job, and he'd always take time to explain to me that getting a job wasn't as rosy as it seems, that there's a lot of responsibility with it. That was in everything but girls—he wouldn't even talk to me about females.

Why not?

Campbell: Well, he always told me that it was my choice to make and I'd have to live with the one that I chose. So he didn't want to interfere at all, 'cause he was afraid that if he put some negative pressure on, I'd just treat him as the villain and treat her as the hero of the story, and even make our short-lived relationship that much better.

What about your mother?

Campbell: She's forty-five, a secretary at a big corporation. Before that she was a clerk.

What kind of person is she?

Campbell: She's a strong lady, as far as being able to hold up pretty well, especially in front of my sister. She's assumed two roles now, and she's accepting that pretty well now, although she did have a hard time at first.

Does she get depressed?

Campbell: Yes, she does.

What about brothers and sisters?

Campbell: I have a sister, seventeen. She's a typical seventeen-year-old—happy, goes to parties a lot, was a cheerleader last year and is a song girl this year.

Does she confide in you?

Campbell: No.

Does she relate well to your mother?

Campbell: Uh . . . no.

In what way?

Campbell: She'll do things in spite of my mother. Like, she'll be placed on restriction so she's not supposed to drive the car and she'll take it someplace anyway.

Do you talk to her?

Campbell: I try to, but she tells me to keep my nose out of her business.

What do you say to her?

Campbell: That's fine. I just don't bother any more, because when I do, it usually causes a big family ruckus, so we just try to stay away from each other as much as possible.

Do you think she'll come around?

Campbell: I think so. When she first started dating, she used to not really know the people she was dating—she'd go out with anybody who asked her, and then she'd chase them. And now she's using a little more discrimination as far as her dating goes.

How did your sister take your father's death?

Campbell: She was crushed. She got along with him pretty well.

Was he pretty lenient with her?

Campbell: No. He was fair to both of us; he gave us both rights.

Tell me more about yourself.

Campbell: I think I'm an easygoing guy. I have no trouble getting along with people, especially with people in the department.

What about people on the street? Blacks, Chicanos, and so forth?

Campbell: I never had any problem with them on patrol. I went to school with Chicanos. We have a black cadet; I get along with him very well.

How did you feel about coming to see me?

Campbell: I felt threatened, because I figured that I was put through the grinder once, and I felt like having just one person recommend that I get the job or not. I felt that was threatening.

What do you think of me now?

Campbell: I think you're intelligent. I know you're intelligent from all the degrees you have. It means you've strived to make yourself better. I don't consider you better than I am, though. [Long silence.]

What are you thinking, John?

Campbell: I'm thinking something I was told: "If Dr. Shev stares at you, grit your teeth, grab your balls, and stare right back."

[*Laughter.*] *Who told you that?*

Campbell: Lieutenant Reynolds. I have a habit . . . when I first started working as a cadet, I was told—in fact, I had a couple of talks with Lieutenant Reynolds about this—that I wasn't looking a person in the eye when I talked to them. I'd look a little to the side, like I was being distracted, but still carrying on a conversation. But I've been working on it, and the lieutenant has helped me with it.

What's important about looking in someone's eyes?

Campbell: Some people feel like you're really not interested in what they have to say or you're really not enthused about what you're saying to them if you're not looking at them.

How superstitious are you?

Campbell: You mean black cats and that kind of thing?

Oh, bad night, good night, full moon, whatever.

Campbell: I'm not very superstitious.

[*Pause.*] *If I stop and look at you, what do you think I'm thinking?*

Campbell: I don't know. Sometimes I think you're trying to psych me out—waiting for me to fall apart.

Why should I want to do that?

Campbell: I guess to test how long I can last under some type of pressure. Well, sometimes I think you want me to go on and elaborate on things, but I don't have more to say. I don't know how to give examples. Sometimes I just have nothing more to add. [Pause.] You asked me about suspicions, and I said, "No, I don't think I'm very suspicious."

But I asked if you were superstitious.

Campbell: Oh, well, that was a mistake on my part, then.

That was a Freudian slip.

Campbell: Very much so.

What are you suspicious about here?

Campbell: I'm not suspicious about anything here.

You said you were.

Campbell: That was a slip, whether it was Freudian or not.

Well, we're going to determine if it was a Freudian slip by having you examine your reasons for saying it.

Campbell: I don't feel suspicious; I'm just very nervous about being here.

What're you nervous about?

Campbell: Passing or failing this examination.

I'm not going to pass or fail you. You know that—I told you that.

Campbell: Yes, but I know your opinion has a great influence on whether I get the job, especially since there is only one position and I am the youngest applicant.

Tell me more about how you got along with your parents.

Campbell: Well, not always that well.

What do you mean, exactly?

Campbell: Well, for a while I went through a stage of consistently lying to my parents; and they were consistently finding out about it. I didn't want them to know where I was going, so I'd say I was going to the library, then go out riding around with some other guys.

That would indicate to me that you were afraid of your parents.

Campbell: I don't feel that I was afraid of them.

Do you think your father's heart attack had something to do with your lying?

Campbell: No.

Do you feel guilty about his death?

Campbell: Yes, I did. I still do sometimes.

What do you think the policeman's role in society is?

Campbell: I think law is made to protect people, not just to punish them. The policeman's role is to keep things neutral in the community.

What are the policeman's discretionary powers for, then?

Campbell: That's part of keeping things neutral—getting the troublemaker out of that place, or out of society. His role is to keep things as quiet as possible in the community. To keep things neutral, you have to keep in check the people that are too far on the left and on the right. Do you understand that? Everything the policeman does—enforcement of traffic laws, enforcement of penal code laws, building ordinances, and everything—is just to keep the city as quiet as possible, without any problems. Which is a dream, but that's his goal.

Do you think his job is to catch criminals?

Campbell: No. In fact, I think that very little of his job is concerned with catching criminals during his tour of duty. One person can't oversee the entire community, or be responsible for it.

What changes would you like to see in the role of police?

Campbell: I want the image to change from one of cops ripping off the public. I think the department I'm associated with is going about it the right way.

This is a psychiatric interview with Robert Halleck, twenty-one, for a patrolman's job. Mr. Halleck is aware that this interview is being taped and that he is to take any questions he has about this meeting to the chief of the department.

What work are you doing now?

Halleck: I'm a full-time student at State—I have a year to go. I also work part time driving a truck.

Why do you want to start work now, if you have only a year to go?

Halleck: I figured I could make it up any time. I want to get into police work. It's interesting.

What's so interesting about it? It's dull, monotonous, full of crap, people yelling at you, screaming at you, spitting on you.

Halleck: It has its drawbacks, but the field is open. It's interesting to me. The different people that you meet; it wouldn't get monotonous to me. After talking to twenty or thirty policemen, their feelings on it—and in school—it's not dull. I'm also a reserve [a reserve gets some training, observes officers while on duty, and is available to assist the department in an emergency or disaster] with the department now; it's good training for me. I can watch officers perform their duties, and in my own mind I can work out which is the best way. I can take a little bit from one man, a little from another, and so on.

What have you learned?

Halleck: What have I learned? Well, we handled a drunk driver one night when I was observing; it was interesting. It improves on what I've learned in school.

Are your parents living?

Halleck: Yes, they are both living and healthy. My father is retired; he was a police officer for thirty years.

What is he like?

Halleck: Well, my father can be hard to get along with at times. He's a minimal drinker; he gets along well with my mother. But he's pretty strict.

Was he an influence on your interest in police work?

Halleck: I think to a small degree, but I was never really pressured. I think as a little kid you always want to grow up and do what your father does, but now I know I want to do it. From school—I started in sociology, didn't like it. I found administration of justice; that's what I was looking for.

Other children in your family?

Halleck: I have three brothers.

What do they do?

Halleck: Two of them are in police work.

Sounds like your father has had a pretty deep influence on his kids.

Halleck: Yes, sir.

Was he a pretty good cop?

Halleck: I would say so, sir. All the reports I've heard—the policemen there liked him.

What about your other brother—what does he do?

Halleck: I don't know exactly what he does. He lives in San Francisco somewhere. He kind of departed from the family—we haven't heard from him in six or seven months. He's doing crafts, I think—something he wanted to do. He had no pressure from the family, though.

Ever hear of unspoken pressure?

Halleck: Yes sir, but I don't think we had it.

Oh? I'm sort of skeptical.

Halleck: [Pause.]

What are you thinking?

Halleck: Well, I was just thinking about why you're skeptical. You probably think I'm pressured into becoming a cop by the family, which I would tend to disagree with.

Well, the only one who isn't a cop dropped out of the family— how do you explain that?

Halleck: He left of his own choosing.

Well, yeah—but I'd have to surmise that he felt the only way he could do something different was to drop out from the family.

Halleck: I don't think so, because he really didn't have any pressure from us.

Do you really expect me to believe that?

Halleck: Yes, sir, 'cause it's the truth.

Then why did he drop out? Was he on drugs?

Halleck: There's never been any solid evidence that he was, but a few people who've seen him recently say there's been a little of it.

How do you feel right now?

Halleck: Nervous—it's my first time seeing a psychiatrist. It's the old cliché—you know, laying down on the couch and everything. When there's something that you haven't been through, then you're nervous about it.

How do you feel about me?

Halleck: What kind of opinion have I formed?

Right—some personal feelings.

Halleck: I really haven't formed an opinion yet.

What kind of person do you think you are?

Halleck: I think I'm a fairly easygoing person. When I decide to do a job, I try to do it as well as I can. I believe I get along well with people. I think I'm a dedicated person.

To what?

Halleck: Right now to getting into police work. I think it's something worth doing.

That doesn't tell me what kind of guy you are. You know, God's gift to society . . . at the moment. . . .

Halleck: I never said I was God's gift to society. Um, like I said, I would be dedicated to my work as a police officer. I get along well with people. I don't know how to put it any other way. I think I'm honest.

Are you a religious person?

Halleck: Well, I'm Catholic. But I don't go to church too often; I try to follow what I was taught in school.

Does religion play a role in law enforcement?

Halleck: As far as arresting a person because he's a Catholic or a Protestant or something, no. But it gives you a sense of morality. I think the officer should have some moral background.

What is the role of the police in society?

Halleck: They protect life and property.

That's a bunch of bull, right out of schoolbooks. I want your answer, your thoughts.

Halleck: Okay, first of all, they're there to keep the people safe in the city. He protects people. Their main function is to protect people and their property from crime in the streets.

The First Candidates / 39

Gee, guess the criminals haven't heard about that, from the way the crime statistics read.

Halleck: But you have a lot more crime now because of drugs.

Because of drugs?

Halleck: Uh-huh.

Do you take any drugs? Alcohol?

Halleck: I drink very little—maybe two beers a week. I tried pot five or six times in high school, but I haven't used it since.

How do you feel about blacks, Jews, et cetera? I mean really feel?

Halleck: Okay, I lived with blacks—grew up in Richmond and had four or five blacks as friends growing up. I try to judge everyone for what he is inside.

How do you feel about being here now?

Halleck: I'm getting a little calmer, a little more at ease. I think I'm hard to psych out. . . .

How do you feel about men?

Halleck: As friends? I have quite a few friends who are men.

How do you feel about homosexuals?

Halleck: I've never come in contact with any of them. That's their business.

This is a psychiatric interview with Alan David Snyder, age twenty-three, for the job of patrolman. Mr. Snyder knows that our conversation is being taped, and he is aware that he should take any questions about the interview to the chief.

Are you working now?

Snyder: Yes, as a clerk in a grocery store, for about a year now.

Why do you want to get into police work?
Snyder: I worked as a campus policeman for two years, and I'm a reserve in the department now. I enjoy the work.
You enjoy lumping all those heads?
Snyder: No, I don't. There are many parts of the job that to me are very satisfying, though. On two occasions I felt that I helped save someone's life, and this was really important to me—it gave me a good feeling. There're other times when I feel that I've helped remove someone from the street who was a menace to other people. Others have a right not to be victimized.
Do you think everyone who breaks a law should be arrested?
Snyder: No. Every day we see minor violations. It's ridiculous to think that you could throw everybody in jail who commits a crime. I think there has to be a certain amount of judgment about who is arrested and who's not.
What's your education?
Snyder: I have my A.A. and fifteen units toward my B.A. . . .
Speak up so I can hear you.
Snyder: [Clears throat, voice still soft.] Yes. I've got my . . . .
Why are you speaking so quietly?
Snyder: Just a little nervous, I guess.
What are you nervous about?
Snyder: Well, this isn't an everyday situation to me—this is something new to me. Uh, I've got fifteen hours toward my B.A. in criminal justice.
What about your mother and father—are they still alive?
Snyder: Yes, they've been married for twenty-eight years, both in good health.
Gee, I can hardly hear you.
Snyder: I'm sorry, I'll try to talk louder.
What's bugging you?
Snyder: Nothing's bug . . . bothering me.

Oh, you know that's not true. You know there's something bothering you.

Snyder: It's just that I'm a little nervous.

What're you so nervous about?

Snyder: Well, like I said before, this is a new situation to me. My getting the job of patrolman hinges on this, among other things, so I'm bound to be nervous. I usually don't speak that loud, but I am a little bit nervous.

Why don't you speak as loud as a normal voice? Why do you whisper so much?

Snyder: I didn't think I was whispering. I don't know, I'm just not loud-spoken.

What's your father do?

Snyder: He's a salesman, travels a lot.

What kind of person is he?

Snyder: To me he expresses a couple different personalities. At times he can be very soft, gentle; at other times he can be very harsh, severe. He's never overly severe—he didn't hit us kids or anything. I think he did a good job of raising the family; and he loves my mother very much.

What are your feelings about police work—the policeman's role in society?

Snyder: Mainly it goes back to the standard of protection of life and property. But I think it's going more toward social work—family disputes and such things. I think social agencies can handle that better; it takes highly specialized training to really work out problems with families. But quite often that's what police do.

How do you feel about minorities, and the fact that they're being hired as police more?

Snyder: I really have mixed emotions on that. One part of me says "Yes, hire the minorities—they have the right to compete with you, throughout the whole gamut of life." But another part of me says, "I don't want to work with someone who's not qualified." I've heard of cases of standards being lowered just because minorities had to be hired.

What should be done?

Snyder: For the immediate problem, I don't think much can be done. Tests are said to favor whites—they should be looked into and changed if that's true. Long range, we should improve education for minorities. I don't think blacks or Chicanos are inferior to me.

What kind of person do you think you are?

Snyder: Well, that's probably the hardest question to answer that I can think of. I think I'm intelligent, I think I have the capabilities to be a police officer. I think I've proven that as a reserve. I'm honest: I think I'm loyal to people that I love. I've got a good control of my temper. I try not to do things impulsively, try not to let my personal feelings interfere with my professionalism in doing my job. I think if I have one fault, it's trying too hard—trying to be too much of a professional, especially in the job that I'm trying to get. That's a job that has very little room for error; I make some, but I try not to.

What do you think the future of police work is?

Snyder: I feel that there'll always be a need for police, as long as there are people who can't control their emotions. Police deal mostly with the lower strata of society, or people who are impulsive, can't control their emotions.

Does a cop deal mostly with troubled people?

Snyder: Other than traffic violations, yes—they've got one type of problem or another. They've been victimized or they're having emotional problems, or physical problems or problems where they feel they should commit a certain crime. So either side of the coin, I think a person is troubled in this type of situation.

That day was one of many times I was glad not to be in the chief's shoes, because I found two of the men qualified for police work. The other man didn't meet the criteria for a good cop, principally because he didn't know his own mind. This other man was Halleck, the second man interviewed; I recommended hiring both Campbell and Snyder. Campbell got the job, but I'm not sure he would have been the one hired if Snyder hadn't become rather seriously ill a few days after his interview with me. Unfortunately, that illness has prevented him from becoming a cop.

My recommendations concerning these men, and all other candidates I interview, are made from the over all picture I can assemble from my conversation with them. Of course each interview is different, but my questions are always aimed at determining certain basic factors, such as a candidate's maturity and his real reasons for pursuing police work.

To achieve this end, I use a specific approach: the psychotherapeutic interview. This technique goes beyond the standard interview, which provides simple psychological evaluation, because I try to provoke a person to demonstrate whether or not he is flexible enough to accept and respond to a psychiatric relationship in which he learns about himself. In my experience, no other form of interview or testing—such as psychometric studies, IQ tests, Rorschach, or personality indexes—can determine a candidate's ability to learn about himself, nor can such studies effectively measure applicants against specific criteria for good policemen.

Among these three men, Campbell shows his flexibility and willingness to learn about himself when he tells of being "coached" by the lieutenant to look into people's eyes during conversations with them. Snyder's candid reply to my question of what kind of person he considers himself—that this is the hardest question for him to answer—shows a similar flexibility and realistic attitude toward himself. Halleck, on the other hand, doesn't take advantage of any opportunity to examine his own feelings, at least in the interview setting. He doesn't pick up on any of the several openings I give him to express his own thoughts about his drop-out brother's situation or the family's role in the brother's departure and the other two sons' interest in police work. Even if he'd say something like, "I'm not sure how I feel about my brother," I'd know that he at least wondered if something was not quite right with his family. Instead, Halleck simply denies the existence of any family pressure.

Halleck's explanation of his own motivation, and his description of the family situation, is a good example of the wrong reasons for going into police work. He seems to be applying for this police job because his father was a cop for thirty years—and the fact that two of his brothers also became policemen bolsters this interpretation. To put it in psychological terms, Halleck is in the *reactive state;* he and his brothers were never given a chance to make a decision about their life's work. They are reacting to the father's wishes, and they will continually be striving unconsciously to please the old man. This is dangerous in a cop, because a person in a reactive state will not make decisions on the street by using independent, objective discretion. As a reactive person, Halleck will make decisions in terms of what he thinks his father would want. He is simply not a free agent. (We can only speculate about the father's motivations, but he probably went into police work by his own decision and with the motivation to help people. And the enthusiasm for the father's type of work among the Halleck brothers is unusual, because the majority of children of police don't want to go into police work.) But for whatever reasons—and we don't know them because he doesn't reveal any personal details—Halleck has been locked into becoming a policeman with no idea and no volition of his own.

Actually, Halleck might be a pretty fair cop on the street because of his textbook idea of police methods and his father's and brothers' influence, assuming that this is a constructive element in his life. But in a sense he'd be a "fake" cop, because his ideas and reactions are not his own, and in a situation of stress or confusion he might fall apart. And the fact that Halleck just didn't respond when I pressed him for something personal represents another aspect of the reactive personality.

The reactive state is one of the two basic terms that can be used to describe general personality states; the other term is *sublimated.* (A person can be described as reactive or sublimated no matter what the specific characteristics of his personality.) A reactive person relates to the world by reacting; like a billiard ball, he reacts by moving—he doesn't move on his own. The person's whole concept of action must come from outside stimuli; nothing is self-generated. The sublimated person, in contrast, is self-generating. He'll stop and think about something before acting. Another distinction between these two personality states is that a sublimated person who confronts the reality of a situation knows what he can do and accepts his limitations, but can be satisfied when doing the work he has chosen. The reactive person can never be satisfied, because he's constantly trying to live up to his frequently unconscious notion of what someone else would like him to be, and he'll never fulfill that objective.

Unlike Halleck's reactive personality, Campbell's and Snyder's can be described as sublimated. Each man reveals a number of personal facts in his interview and makes forthright admissions that could be embarrassing. For instance, Campbell repeats the "stare-right-back" phrase and then volunteers the information about his habit of not looking someone in the eyes. This is a small weakness, but one that he accepts and wants to improve on. And Snyder's rather thorough self-assessment shows that he is reflective, even in a situation where he is admittedly quite nervous. His awareness that he has a possibly volatile temper, which must be kept under control, shows an ability to learn about himself and a willingness to change his behavior.

Closely related to whether a candidate is reactive or sublimated is his degree of maturity. One question I always ask to help me determine this is, "What sort of person do you think you are?" This is usually the most difficult question for candidates to answer, although most of them don't acknowledge that. Usually only the most mature applicants will say right off that self-estimation is a struggle. Of course Snyder is very direct in answering that question, and he has a more mature assessment of himself than either Campbell or Halleck. Both of their answers are rather noncommittal—"I think I'm easygoing, get along well with people," and so forth. Even when I pushed Halleck for a more personal statement by asking if he was "God's gift to society," I couldn't get a thoughtful comment from him.

Other aspects of these interviews also reveal the candidates' maturity or lack of it. One clear-cut example is Campbell's attitude toward his sister. Instead of taking over the role of the deceased father and trying to run her life, he's remaining in the role of a brother. He also makes cogent comments about his sister's situation, such as her dating habits and her rebellion against the mother. This mature attitude toward his family relationships is very important, because a cop has to be able to make an observation without getting emotionally caught up in it. And if he doesn't get caught in the trap with his sister emotionally, Campbell is not going to get caught in the trap of people on the street. In other words, the policeman who is caught in the emotional trap of family problems will project those attitudes—whatever they are—to the people with whom he has to deal in his job.

If Campbell had answered differently, with something like, "Look, I don't give a damn what my sister says about keeping my nose out of her business, I'm going to . . . after all, I am her brother, and I'm older and I know better." This is an authoritarian attitude, and that's what you don't need in the police business. These sorts of attitudes are what I want to reveal by asking a candidate about his relationships within the family. As one of my professors used to say, "Your first battle in life is with your family." And this is how you work out your relationships with the rest of the world—by transferring the ways you relate to your siblings, parents, aunts and uncles, and anyone else in the family constellation.

Campbell also shows some immaturity in the interview, when he responds by telling me, "I think you're trying to psych me out . . . I think you want me to elaborate, but I don't have more to say." This statement suggests a lack of self-assurance, a hint that perhaps I may find out that he is crazy in some way that Campbell himself hasn't realized. His inability to elaborate on his ideas and feelings also shows a concreteness, which is characteristic of many people who go into police work. Things are right or wrong to many cops—that's why they can enforce the laws.

If Campbell had this concreteness to an extreme degree, he might have said, "I don't think there are any more answers—that's all there is" about whatever he was asked to explain further. If he had given that sort of answer, then I'd have probed to find out how rigid he really was. I'd ask such a candidate if he has fantasies, what kinds of things he imagines. If he'd responded that he had none or couldn't understand my questions, I would be alerted to a real inflexibility in this man.

But Campbell's actual response is in effect saying, "I'm really sort of stuck, because I'm not practiced in fantasizing." Although they may seem unrelated, concreteness and fantasizing are really two sides of the same coin. When asked to describe a tree, for example, the "concrete" person would say something like, "It's a brown trunk with branches, with green leaves." He might not think of anything else to say about the tree. The person who is able to fantasize, however, could visualize the tree in other forms as well. He might describe the yellow and red of autumn leaves, the winter's bare branches, a bird's nest hidden among spring blossoms, even the lumber and sawdust if the tree were harvested. Both men are thinking realistically, but only one of them is able to elaborate on the many possibilities of this real object.

Campbell's desire to elaborate shows that he is aware of his concreteness and has some insight into it. At age twenty, though, if he's properly guided in police work from now on, he's going to be able to mature and learn to think imaginatively. (In fact, this is what I suggested in my recommendation to the chief—that Campbell should be placed with a good training sergeant who could supervise and guide him during his first year of service if he were hired.) The important thing about Campbell at this point is that he has a vague sensation that he should be able to elaborate and give examples of his ideas, which is a sign of the flexibility I'm looking for.

Snyder's maturity is apparent in his answer to my question about his attitudes toward minorities. He frankly reveals his mixed feelings about the hiring of minority police, stating that philosophically he's in favor of improved opportunities for blacks, Chicanos, and others, but in practice he wonders if the standards have not been lowered so that minority candidates can be added to police departments. Similarly, Snyder answers most questions without any pretense, as when he acknowledges that describing himself is very difficult.

Halleck's refusal to reveal any of his real feelings about his family, his own attitude toward police work, and his brother's departure from home may indicate immaturity to the point of not being able to cope with his own emotions or confusion. Instead, it seems easier for him just to go along with what he thinks is expected by his father and two brothers who are cops.

Another important measure of a candidate's maturity and openness is my asking what he thinks of me. I'm an authoritarian figure to him, a parental figure who seems to him to have yes or no power over him in the form of a job. So I try to get the candidate to express how afraid he really is in this setting—being quizzed by a shrink who practically holds the man's job in his hands. And I try to determine whether a person will give me credit for being fair with him or whether he will be prejudiced against me and make me the villain. I'm interested in seeing if he can face the reality of the situation—his nervousness and my influence in his being hired or not. I also try to communicate to him that he is in a dynamic situation in which he has to keep participating. If a candidate is so petrified of me that he can't keep the interview alive, then he shouldn't be a cop, because he will be dealing with authoritarian figures all the time, and he must be one himself, as part of the job.

Each of the three candidates here responds differently to this question. Halleck cops out totally, refusing to deal with the issue by saying that he hasn't formed any opinion of me as yet. Snyder is very nervous; he acknowledges the importance of our interview to his getting the job, and he is a bit defensive when asked what's bothering him. But he doesn't back down, even when interrupted with my questions about his soft voice. Campbell at first doesn't acknowledge his apprehension of our interview, but in the discussion of his Freudian slip about "suspicion/superstition," he does admit that he's worried about my opinion of him. He knows that my recommendations have been influential with the chief in the past, and he is particularly anxious about my assessment of him because he is the youngest of the three candidates vying for one position. Yet Campbell is relaxed enough with me to repeat the lieutenant's comment, which suggests that he is able to cope with an authoritarian figure. This is one reason why I felt that he is basically a solid person.

Campbell's Freudian slip is a good example of the kind of opportunity I can use to follow through in the interview situation, to keep the candidate on the hot seat. And this is necessary because I have to get the maximum information and reaction from a person in a fifty-minute session. These applicants are not patients; they're not supposed to be. One value of the psychotherapeutic interview is that I know nothing about the candidate—I have to learn everything from his answers and attitudes when he's in the room with me. So I take every opportunity to explore the areas that may indicate special problems or abilities. (In contrast, if a patient had made a slip such as Campbell's using the word "suspicion" when he meant "superstition," I wouldn't confront him. I'd say something like, "Gee, that was an interesting slip of the tongue you made," and let it drop. Then I'd bring it up at a subsequent session, perhaps several months later. And we'd explore it, rather than my challenging him about it.)

Sometimes my probing looks like badgering, as when I told Halleck that his definition of the police function was out of a schoolbook or pressed Snyder to speak up. But my pushing the candidate has a purpose, because a person in the interview situation is under the gun to react in almost the same way as a cop in any kind of tense situation on the street. He has to react instantly, yet he must think about his options and come up with logical answers that are meaningful for his situation.

Finally, I always ask candidates some questions that relate directly to their potential work as police. My standard opener is, "What is the role of police in society?", a subject they should have thought out thoroughly by the time they reach my office for screening. Very often a candidate will give the textbook answer—"to protect life and property." Few cops see their function in its more appropriate, larger context—to preserve the established power structure. Yet that is what most candidates are implying when they say such things as "their role is to keep things neutral."

Another topic that pertains to a policeman's everyday work is his attitudes about other races and religions—in short, his prejudices. This is one question that candidates consistently avoid answering honestly. They usually say that they don't think they are prejudiced, that they get along well with the minority members of the department or they grew up with blacks and Chicanos. As in their definition of the police function in society, candidates tend to give stereotyped answers—"some of my best friends are. . . ." I usually don't pursue this question, because that answer in itself tells me that they are probably prejudiced. Yet prejudice should not rule out someone as a potential cop. If the candidate's personality is sublimated, he will still have his prejudice, but he will be aware of it when carrying out his responsibilities on the street. In fact, this person will bend over backward not to be abusive, because he's conscious of his attitudes.

The person I'm suspicious about, though, is the man who says to me, "I can work with *anybody*," because none of us can work with everybody. I try to pursue this by asking about the man's background—what sort of neighborhood he grew up in, if it was integrated, how he got along with the other kids there, and so forth. Sometimes the way he describes the situation will give me an inkling of how prejudiced he is and whether his attitudes are so rigid that he can't be objective when dealing with certain people. If I can't really get much information about a person's attitudes, I assume that he has some prejudice. Then I examine this assumption in light of the other things I know about him—such as whether or not he has given candid, personal answers to other questions—to determine the possible effect of prejudice on his work as a cop.

Prejudice, concepts of police in society, family background, self-assessment—all go into the composite portrait I make from my interview with a candidate. Of course some of those deductions come from what the person *doesn't* say, or from his gestures, posture, and appearance. I want to see, for instance, how an applicant handles the stress of the interview, so I shift the burden to him—he has to break the silence or retain his composure if I push him for his true feelings. Each person reacts differently: Halleck resisted to the end, Snyder's voice was a whisper at first, Campbell made a Freudian slip. When I measure each of these portraits against the characteristics of a good cop and the criteria for ruling out major psychological or emotional problems, I can make a cogent recommendation to the chief.

3
Selecting a New Chief

FOR A YEAR I interviewed and evaluated the Campbells and Hallecks and Snyders, telling the chief—in essence—"yes," "no," or "yes, but" about each one. By early 1966 I had talked with forty men, and more than half of them (twenty-two) were in the borderline "yes, but" category. Four others were definitely suitable for police work, six were poor risks whom I recommended against hiring, and eight had obvious psychological or emotional problems that ruled them out as police.

These proportions of stable, borderline, and unstable police applicants have generally held true throughout my years of screening: a few are excellent prospects, about a third are unacceptable, and the large majority is basically all right but often in need of some extra guidance. Since working extensively with several departments, I've also found that working cops can be classified into three definite categories. The "natural" cops constitute only 5 per cent of all police; these are men and women who know intuitively how to handle both the work and the pressures of being a cop. Their own personalities form the basis for the confidence and discretion that police work requires daily, and they seem to absorb the cop's detailed knowledge and training almost as if they knew it all beforehand.

The second category comprises 60 per cent of all police, the "treatable" cops. Most of the time these persons perform their duties well, but they have to work hard to master all the skills of being a police officer. More important, each man or woman in this majority has a breaking point, an aspect to his or her personality that may jeopardize police and citizens in a situation of extreme pressure or under just the right combination of forces. Yet these basically healthy cops can perform as capably as the "naturals" if they are encouraged to recognize their weaknesses and to overcome their tendency to overreact under the pressures that affect them adversely.

But the really dangerous police are the 35 per cent who make up the third category. These are the "untreatable" men and women—the bad cops. Their personalities are not suited to police work, and they are unable to learn about themselves or accept treatment that would allow them to function adequately as police officers. One cop in three is untreatable, and the actions of this minority are usually responsible for the bad reputation of police in many communities.

During that first year I began to feel some of the frustrations of being a consultant. I was outside the police department, offering my independent judgments to the chief. And inevitably, we disagreed on some candidates. Several men I had recommended against were hired anyway, and some borderline applicants were taken on without any provision for the special guidance I had suggested. Of course the chief considered a number of factors in deciding which men to hire; my opinions were only a part of the package.

I didn't want to change my status as consultant—the chief

and city officials wouldn't have given me veto power in any case—but I felt that some sort of follow-up was necessary. Psychiatric screening of applicants would have the greatest value to the department if the cops who needed individual guidance and counseling could get it. And I knew that perhaps a third of the officers who had been hired without any psychiatric screening were not suited to this work; yet there were no methods for identifying these cops or channeling them into other, less pressured jobs. So by the end of my first year as a consultant I was ready to propose a new component of in-service training for the department.

I arranged a luncheon meeting with the Sausalito mayor, Mel Wax, to discuss the idea. We met in San Francisco, because my office was there and he covered city government for the San Francisco *Chronicle*. I arrived at the restaurant first; Wax came in about ten minutes later, looking as if he'd just come in out of the rain.

"Sorry I'm late, Ed. I got caught in a fracas at city hall— some demonstrators were picketing in front of the main entrance, and the police detail kept trying to clear a path to the door. One cop got a bullhorn and warned them several times to let people pass, but they just ignored him. Finally he just flipped out: he grabbed a fire hose from one of the wall outlets, turned it on, and charged the demonstrators. Everybody within twenty yards of the entrance got soaked—we were just too surprised to move. I couldn't believe a well-trained city cop would pull a stunt like that."

I laughed at the thought of an angry cop shooting water at a bunch of demonstrators and reporters, but I wasn't surprised. This was precisely the sort of volatile reaction some police have to a highly frustrating situation—I'd read about many such incidents, and I'd seen a few myself. And this was precisely what I wanted to avoid among Sausalito police; Wax couldn't have given me a better justification for a departmental psychiatric training program if he'd looked all year.

I described my proposed in-service program, which would go beyond screening of applicants to include regular, ongoing discussions and counseling designed to keep the Sausalito cops cool under pressure.

"What I have in mind is a three-part program. I'd give a talk once a month on a subject that's relevant to police work, such as the effects of drugs and alcohol, how to handle people under the influence of drugs, or how to deal with street people. Then I'd be available for group therapy once a month, too: this would be more casual, something I'd call a bull session. And finally, I'd give individual counseling to any officer who requests it or is referred to me by the chief."

"Uh-huh, but . . ." Wax paused, "you're going to catch hell from lots of people for suggesting that our police need a shrink."

"I know, but this is a gap that needs to be filled. Even though California has the nation's highest educational standards for police, few cops have been sufficiently trained in psychology or sociology. In most cases, they react to human situations by intuition. A lot of their actions are governed by the attitudes passed along by their families. If those intuitions and attitudes aren't healthy ones, it's too bad for the citizens and for the cops."

"I agree that some of our officers could benefit from the sort of training and counseling you propose. But I'm afraid you're going to have a real struggle convincing some of the men, not to mention the council, that you're anything but a liability."

"Well, I've been that route plenty of times—some of them will never accept me. But if a few men are receptive, most of the others will get something out of these sessions, even if they don't realize it at the time."

Wax also expressed concern about the cost of such a program. He warned me that the council was reluctant to spend anything not previously included in the city's appropriations, and this might sway them to decline this new

Selecting a New Chief / 57

program. I told him that the cost wouldn't be high and that I'd submit an exact figure in a few days. The mayor suggested that I give that budget to Brown, the city manager, before the next council meeting. Wax also asked that I attend that session and present my proposal for the in-service training program.

I had about ten days before the confrontation to devise reasonable answers to all the possible questions and figure out the cost of this program. When I called Brown the next week, he was pleased to hear that my budget for the whole program was only $1200 for a year—and he said he'd go to bat for it. I was ready, too, and enthusiastic about proposing a program that could offer an important new addition to police training.

But the police chief pulled the rug out from under me. Just two days before I was to meet with the council, Huck submitted his resignation; he had been hired away by another city. Brown phoned to tell me this and to ask if I'd interview applicants for Huck's job. He also added that we'd have to hold off on my proposal until a new chief was hired. So instead of explaining and perhaps beginning the psychiatric in-service program, I would be screening the final candidates for a new chief.

Huck left a month later, and Brown appointed a lieutenant on the force as acting chief. This man also applied for the permanent job, although the search for a chief was concentrated outside the department. The memory of the uproar over the selection and later firing of Huck's predecessor was still fresh, and the mayor and city manager were determined to seek highly qualified candidates.

The job requirements were quite specific: at least two years of college, six years in police work with three at the rank of sergeant or above; additional college work could be substituted for some years of experience. More than fifty men applied for the job. After background investigations, interviews with the city manager, and oral exams by a board of citizens and police, the field was narrowed to four men, all of whom I was to interview.

My screening would be the last phase of the hiring process. I would prepare a report on each finalist and rank them in order of preference, based on my interviews; the mayor, city manager, and council members would do the same, based on the men's references, experience, and oral exams. We were all to meet on the last Saturday in May to make our recommendations from which the council would select the new chief.

The Sausalito council chambers dated from another era—dark paneling, heavy oak table and chairs, even a wooden-bladed overhead fan. These surroundings seemed an unlikely setting in which to start something new and progressive, especially in terms of police recruitment and counseling procedures—or even the selection of the chief. The council members' personalities and politics ranged from liberal to almost reactionary, and included the shades in between. I had no idea how they would come to agreement on a new police chief, but this meeting promised to be interesting.

Since all of the council members had not met all four candidates, Brown gave a brief description of each finalist:

"John Bolton is thirty-seven years old, has fifteen years' experience in police work, and is currently training director of a large police department in southern California. He has an A.A. degree plus twenty units of additional police science courses. He is divorced but will marry again soon. In our interview he seemed self-assured and said he wants to leave the smog and crowded living conditions of southern California and to work in a smaller department than his present one. His references are good, but not outstanding.

"John Hawkins is thirty-one, with five years as a patrolman and three as a sergeant. He's bright and has a B.A. in police science; currently he is training sergeant for a small city in this area. He is married and has two children. He has a forceful, decisive manner and his references say he's conscientious.

"Edward Kreins is thirty-two, has been a policeman for ten years, and has six years of college—a B.A. in sociology and another in police science. He set up and runs the training program for a medium-sized department. He's married, with a family. He is very straightforward, says what he thinks. His chief reports that he is competent and thoughtful.

"Bill Turner is twenty-nine, with six years in police work; he has two years of college. He has moved up rather quickly in his department and has served as deputy chief and acting chief at various times. He is single. He's quite intelligent and, according to his references, is well liked and a hard worker."

Wax took a poll of the council to get their preferences and found that Turner, the single man who'd served as an acting chief, was the strong favorite. Then the mayor asked Brown and me our opinions; we both ranked Kreins first and Turner fourth.

The surprise on several members' faces quickly turned to consternation. "Why did you put Turner last?" one man demanded. "He made lieutenant in three years and is very popular with the men. And everything went smoothly during the three months he was acting chief of his department."

"My assessment," I reminded the council, "is based on a psychotherapeutic interview with this man. During that session I found Turner to be emotionally unstable and a potential addict of some kind, possibly an alcoholic; he is unable to relate well to women, which suggests that he would have difficulty being a mature husband or father. In fact, I believe his emotional problems may be so severe that he shouldn't even be a cop."

This statement shocked everyone, and I remember thinking, "At this point they're all wondering whether *I'm* the one who's off base, instead of Turner." Brown and Wax spoke at the same instant, so that neither could be heard. They paused, and Brown tried again. "I just want to say that I agree with Dr. Shev. Turner seemed immature to me, and my conversations with others in his department indicate to me that he has gone far only because his primary goal is to be liked, rather than to be a good cop or a decisive leader."

Wax's voice rose to drown out the exchanges among the other members. "Since Dr. Shev is our psychiatric consultant, let's hear his assessments of the other three men before we go any further." There were nods of assent, and six faces turned toward me.

"All right, you've heard my opinion of Turner. As for Hawkins, the training sergeant, he is an authoritarian, military type of officer, the sort of cop who goes by the book no matter what and thinks he knows the acceptable moral code of behavior for everybody. But beneath his hard-nosed exterior, this candidate is not the strong man he appears to be; in a tight situation or under stress, I don't think he would be an effective leader."

"Kreins is the most mature and has a good sense of himself and his abilities. He is willing to say what he thinks and will stick to a decision even if criticized for it. Yet he is willing to listen to other opinions and relates well to his colleagues. He has the best education and technical training of the candidates, as well as a strong sense of the role of a police department and how to fulfill its obligations to the community.

"Finally, Bolton has applied for this job to get away from the source of his previous marital failure in southern California. He has a new girl here, and he wants to make a fresh start. His interest in police work is only secondary. He had no specific suggestions for this department and no clear sense of why he went into law enforcement, even though he has lots of experience. This job would just be a convenient new setting for him."

The room was quiet for a few moments, as several members

looked for evidence among their notes and copies of the men's applications. One member finally spoke: "I agree with your opinion of Bolton. I sensed that he really didn't care about this job, but of course the information we have didn't tell us the whole story."

One of the councilors who had ranked Turner first spoke next. "Your comments on the other three applicants had to do with their ideas about police work and their leadership potential. But what you said about Turner almost sounds like slander. How can you judge if he's a potential alcoholic? Who cares if he's a lousy family man? Aren't we supposed to judge a person on his work?"

Here was the suspicion of my role that I've come to expect in such circumstances. But it also was a chance to tell the council more about my approach to working with the Sausalito police. "You're really asking me three things: who am I to judge these men; what kind of man does it take to be a cop or police chief; and what do the facts about Turner—at work and elsewhere—tell us about his potential to be chief? First, as a psychiatrist I base these judgments on the whole of my interview with a person—his responses, his expressions and posture, his attitudes toward me and toward the subjects we discuss, as interpreted from my training and experience with similar subjects and people.

"Second, my interviews and other research have demonstrated that a cop has to be a certain kind of person. Because he is armed—with weapons and with authority to arrest or detain—he has to be emotionally stable and healthy. And he must be able to keep his cool under severe stress, more so than in any other occupation. So I try to determine a man's potential for coming unglued as well as his basic personality and motivation.

"Now, Turner is something of a special case. He is not just a poor candidate for chief; his psychological problems make him potentially dangerous as a policeman right now. My assessment is based on his comments about his family, his feelings about women, his general demeanor, and his attitude toward police work. Incidentally, he felt that the department was doing fine and had no ideas for changes or improvements. I didn't mention that in my earlier description because I felt that his questionable emotional status was of paramount importance in the council's consideration of this man."

The man who had prompted my explanation sat quietly, looking at the papers in front of him, but another council member commented. "That all seems plausible to me—it just shows how a likable and apparently average guy can be something very different underneath."

"Exactly," I added. "And we should bear in mind that a cop must be *more* than an average guy, because of the special nature of his position in our community."

"Let's talk some more about Kreins," suggested a member who had originally ranked Turner first. Brown offered his opinion: "I found this man to have a strong personality and convictions. He's the candidate who will give me the most trouble, because he'll always be fighting for better facilities and more jobs in his department. That's precisely why he's my choice for chief; I know he'll really work at improving the police force. He certainly won't be a caretaker or political 'yes man'."

The members discussed Kreins's background and the two people who'd interviewed him offered their assessments, describing him as blunt but straightforward and confident. After a lengthy discussion, during which the council again explored my role in the selection process, the special pressures of all police officers from patrolman to chief, and the need for a strong, independent leader in the department, the vote was unanimous: Ed Kreins became the new police chief.

I felt gratified to have participated in this process, and to have seen superficial judgments—or at least the urge to appoint someone who was popular and could "get along"—

take a back seat to thorough psychiatric examination. Indeed, I felt then, in May 1966, that I had contributed to an uncommon civic event, the thorough screening and objective selection of a city police chief. Today that event is even more rare, because the people who make these decisions are prey to so many factions—civil service officials; police officers' unions; citizens' pressure groups, prosecutors, judges, and lawyers; and the mass of voters, who always control a politician's future. Certainly some good chiefs are chosen, but usually only if a mayor or city council has rejected the politically expedient course of action. All too often, though, political considerations dominate, and the department and ultimately the people suffer for it.

The Sausalito council had picked a highly qualified chief, and now they were about to be introduced to a whole new concept as well—my proposal for a psychiatric in-service program for the entire department. And despite my apparent influence in the group's consideration of candidates for chief, I knew that the notion of approving and funding a shrink for the police would be a lot harder for these five people to swallow. This time I'd have to contend with both politics and their private apprehensions about psychiatry.

Wax introduced me when the council reconvened after a short break.

"As you know, I've been interviewing police candidates for the past year and a half, and I think we've made some real progress in choosing the best men for the force. But I also believe that our society, particularly our city, is entering into turbulent times. You know, lots of people think Sausalito is just a ritzy suburb of San Francisco—another Darien or Grosse Point. But we're not a suburb at all—Sausalito is fundamentally an urban community: we have light and heavy industry, a fishing fleet and marine businesses, a thriving artists' community, and even a company that is reputed to make pornographic films. We have an affluent white community that wants safety and order in the city; we have a sizable and increasingly assertive black community next door; and we're about to begin busing children to desegregate the schools that serve both of these groups. We have runaway kids smoking pot and camping out in our parks, and on weekends we have thousands of tourists to manage, besides. All this means that we need the coolest, most stable cops on our streets or we could have some very serious problems. You know the sort of thing I mean—racial incidents, charges of police brutality, maybe even mob violence. To put it bluntly, we're sitting on a powder keg.

"What I'm suggesting is that we help keep our police cool by offering them special training and counseling. My part in this would be to give a monthly talk to the department on something they have to deal with often, such as drug addiction, alcoholism, runaway kids, tense racial situations, and so on. I would also meet the men between shifts once a month for what I hope would be an all-out bull session; they could talk about specific cases, or blow off steam, or just ignore me if they wished. And I'd be available for individual counseling for any member of the force who desired it."

"Those people out on the streets who are bugging the police need a psychiatrist a lot worse than our cops do," one councilor objected.

City Manager Brown responded to this comment, agreeing that many of the citizens could indeed benefit from psychiatric help, but pointing out that the police should have the best possible preparation to deal with those very people. "I can't argue with that," the man answered, "but do we need a psychiatrist to supply that training? Don't the police academies and training officers know their jobs? Doesn't this new chief Dr. Shev is so high on know his job? No offense, Doctor, but we'll be the laughingstock of Marin County if we start something like this."

"New ideas are usually laughed at," I replied. "But we're

talking about an experiment that could give the city better police—men who will handle themselves with composure and treat citizens with some understanding as well as respect. More important, judicious counseling of some officers might defuse a time bomb or two—and believe me, we have a few in our department now."

"Are you suggesting that the screening hasn't worked?" someone asked. "No," I said, "I'm saying that some of the police who weren't screened might not have passed that test, and most recruits could benefit from follow-up evaluation and guidance during their first year on the force. But in a way you're right, because two men have been hired who didn't get my recommendation. That makes the in-service program even more essential to the department. And I can't repeat this often enough, so let me say it once again: we are not talking about average civil servants, we are talking about police officers, the only people society allows to use guns at their own discretion to enforce our laws. Not only do we have to select those who are uncommonly stable and mature, we also have to stick with them, help them handle the extraordinary pressures of their job."

The one member who hadn't commented yet, the man who'd been most strongly in favor of hiring Turner, flipped through the applications still in front of him, then pitched them into the center of the table. "I feel as if I've been hoodwinked," he said angrily. "Here you gave us these psychological ditties about the candidates for chief, damning the man three of us liked best. Now we find out that you're pushing a whole psychiatric program for the department. Does that mean you shoved Kreins at us because he'll go along with this scheme?"

"Nobody's trying to fool anybody," I answered, angry myself. "I proposed this program in detail to Mel before Chief Huck resigned—and we only delayed discussing it here because the department had no permanent chief."

"That's right," Wax interrupted, "I said that at the beginning of this discussion."

"But you're correct about one thing," I resumed. "I did ask all four candidates about a psychiatric in-service program for the department. Bolton, Hawkins, and Turner said 'Fine, sounds great,' or something similar. They were lying—none of them wanted to be there, in my office, being questioned about their personal lives. How could they endorse me so glibly for their future department? Those men were just responding in the way they thought I'd approve. Only Kreins gave me an honest answer; he said, 'Well, maybe—if you can show me it's beneficial and if it doesn't take money away from other things the department needs.'

"I'm not interested in playing politics with this council, or in putting anything over on you. I've based my assessment of our police and my proposal on the screening interviews and the men who've been hired in the last year. I hope that you'll consider the proposal on that basis—not because these two matters just happened to come up on the same day."

Wax backed me up. "The fact that we're taking up this psychiatric program today is really only a matter of convenience. You're here, Ed, and we've benefited from your assistance in our selection of a chief. And we both know that there's been no conspiracy or scheming—I'm sure the council will examine the merits of your program and give it a fair hearing."

The mayor spoke confidently, implying to the other councilors that he considered them above any questionable motives or vindictiveness. I hoped he was right.

There was another strained silence, which was finally broken by the mayor. "Let's get down to practical details, Ed. How long would the program last, and how much would it cost?" I explained that my proposal was for a year and consisted of my spending four hours per month with the men and being available as needed for private sessions. The cost would be $1200 for the year.

Brown spoke up, noting that he could probably find federal money or a foundation grant to cover the program's budget. But I objected to this. "If someone else's money is funding this project, then I won't be responsible to you or to the department—it will be forms and reports and some outsider looking over our shoulders. The city should fund it, because then it will be your program, and we can change or add to it, without jeopardizing our support. Besides, I will be accepted much more readily by the police if I'm officially part of their budget, and therefore part of their department."

Brown looked at me, smiled, and said, "You don't go halfway, do you?"

"No," I smiled back, "I guess I'm just a bit compulsive." That remark brought laughter from everybody and visibly eased the tension in the room.

"Are there any more questions for Dr. Shev?" the mayor asked. No one spoke, so Wax continued. "You know we can't make any appropriation until it's been considered at two meetings, so we'll put this on next week's agenda and make a decision then." I thanked the council and asked the members to call me if they had further questions during the week. The council moved on to its other business, and I moved out into the bright afternoon. I was not at all sure what would have been decided by this time next Saturday.

4
The Program Begins

THE NEXT WEEK seemed endless. During those six days between council meetings I realized how important this work had become to me. And I hoped the council understood that we'd be pioneering a whole new aspect of police work through this program—the development of police who are informed about their own and others' behavior, who are capable of making sound decisions under intense pressure, and who can remain cool in the turbulent, emotional situations that have become almost routine to city life. Several times I resisted the impulse to phone Wax or Brown to ask their opinion of the program's chances; instead I planned answers to new questions I anticipated from council members. But their calls never came.

Saturday finally came, though, and the waiting was down to hours. I knew that Brown would phone me as soon as the meeting was adjourned, so I went to my study to catch up on paper work until then. I tried to imagine the discussion going on in that antiquated council room and wished I had said more last week or could be there to say more today. It wasn't just that I wanted to help improve police performance, although that was my main objective. But I also felt that I'd benefit from involvement with such a community project. One of the most deadening aspects of psychiatry is the isolation of the psychiatrist from his community. His work consists of one-to-one relationships with troubled people, and he rarely deals with them in a larger context. I have always believed that psychiatrists must get off their duffs and out into the community if they are truly in a service profession. I was convinced that if the Sausalito council approved it, we could have a program for police that would be useful for everybody.

The phone rang before I'd done much paper work. "Well, it was something of a tussle," Charles Brown said, "but the program went through."

"Thanks, Charlie—that's great. You'll have to tell me the details."

"Can't talk now, Ed—we're just on a break from the meeting. Besides, I may save this episode for my memoirs."

So the program had cleared its biggest hurdle—or so I thought. Kreins was slated to take over as chief in a few weeks, and I hoped we could get things under way before my August vacation. He was familiar with the screening process and we had briefly discussed the possibility of an in-service program in our interview. In fact, everything I knew about Ed Kreins indicated that he'd be open-minded and fair in implementing the psychiatric program for the department.

In early July I called Kreins to discuss topics and scheduling for the program. He asked that we hold off until he felt more at home among the men, and I reluctantly agreed to wait a few more weeks. During that month I was not contacted to interview any new candidates.

I was out of town for the month of August, and one of my first calls after returning was to Chief Kreins. To my dismay, he hedged about starting the program, saying that the department had urgent needs for equipment and he didn't

70 / GOOD COPS/BAD COPS

see how he could justify this experiment to his men. When I reminded him that the council had approved the program, Kreins said he was aware of it; then he asked if I'd call him next week to arrange a meeting. His tone of voice left no room for argument, so I replied that he'd be sure to hear from me.

At that point I was frustrated and disappointed—I hadn't expected opposition from Ed Kreins. Later that day I was plain furious, when I learned from Mel Wax that Kreins had hired five men while I was away. None of them had been screened.

Wax got the brunt of my anger: "This is just too much! This morning Kreins told me he doesn't want to start the 'experiment' because the department needs equipment, and now I find out that he has finessed me completely. We can't have a screening program that only screens the chief's rejects. And it looks as if we can't have an in-service program at all."

"You're right, Ed, we can't screen some men and exempt others. Kreins seems to have overstepped his authority here. I think the best thing would be for the three of us to sit down and get this straightened out. That way we can deal with both the screening and the expanded program. How about next Wednesday?"

"A little sooner would suit me, but that date is all right if there's nothing earlier."

I didn't prepare any speeches for the Wednesday confrontation. I knew that if I thought too much about the chief's apparent disregard for our procedures I'd go into that meeting loaded for bear. And that would be no way for two strong personalities—Kreins's and mine—to come to an understanding. But I did want some answers.

We met in the council chambers—it was the most neutral territory. Wax and Kreins were there when I arrived, already discussing the chief's request for a bigger police budget. The talk stopped as I entered.

"Hi, Ed," Wax opened. "The chief and I were just

The Program Begins / 71

bemoaning the usual state of affairs—too little money."

"Yes, I know the problem, but at the moment I'm more concerned about people. Chief," I sat down across from Kreins and looked straight at him, "how does it happen that you hired five new men without sending them through the screening process?"

"Well, Dr. Shev, I was under the impression that you were only supposed to interview the ones with no prior police experience or the men we had some question about. But those men are all experienced officers, and I'm familiar with their work."

"My impression is that our screening procedure was explained to you quite clearly—by me in our interview and later by Charles Brown. So I can't go along with your explanation. Isn't it more likely that you just resented having me consult on these men, because you thought they were great and you didn't want to hear otherwise?"

Kreins stared back at me and pushed his chair away from the table. It was a full ten seconds before he replied—I could've sworn he was counting them off. "You may have a point, Doctor, although I wasn't really thinking that way at the time. But I knew you were away, and besides, I'm the one with ten years' experience in police work. I ought to be able to choose men who are good for the jobs we need done." He paused for breath, and his face flushed just a little. "To tell the truth, what I resent is the implication that I can't make a sound decision." The red got a little redder.

"We're not suggesting that you don't know police work or the department's needs," Wax spoke up, before I could contradict the chief. "But you're also experienced enough to know that city government—just like most of police work—has to be played by the book. If not, we have chaos. And Dr. Shev is in the book."

"And, Ed," I turned to Kreins, "if we're going to argue we might as well use first names—I'm afraid you don't know how to spot all the problems, because at least one of your new sergeants is pretty mixed up. I deduced that in five minutes' conversation with him on the street the other day. God knows what we may find out about the others."

In fact, I found out later that three of the five men Kreins had hired were unstable; the one I'd mentioned was definitely not suited for police work, and two others had emotional problems that could threaten their behavior and thus endanger the public as well as other cops. The remaining two men were basically all right. All five remained in police work for a number of years; the two stable men are currently chiefs of small departments, but the other three have gone sour.

"Which man do you mean?" Kreins demanded. I named him, and the chief was incredulous. "I don't believe it!" he almost shouted. "I've worked with that man for two years—he's smart, efficient, and dedicated. I don't see how you could find some big psychological hang-ups in a five-minute talk with him."

"Nevertheless, I did."

"Wait a minute," Wax cut in. "Aren't all new employees considered probationary until they've been with us for a year? So you could do an evaluation of these particular men before they're made permanent, couldn't you, Ed?"

"Yes, and I intend to watch them closely," I said. "But that won't take the place of screening—it will be harder on them and on us if we have to dismiss any of them after they've been on the force for a while."

I paused to give Kreins a chance to speak, but he stayed quiet, looking rather sullen. So I addressed him: "How about it—if I find any of these men unsuitable—through interviews and observation—will you follow my recommendation and not make them permanent?"

"I can't say now whether I will or I won't. I'll consider your opinion, but if I think they're doing well, I probably

The Program Begins / 73

won't can them on your say-so. And where did this evaluation business come from, anyway? This is the first time I've heard of that angle."

"Look," I replied, "we have an established procedure. You take a candidate through the test and oral interview, then I interview him, then you decide whether to hire him. I'm not trying to add another stage to that process—I'm just insisting that we use the machinery we already have. And now that machinery includes the in-service program, with my lectures and small group sessions and some individual counseling. The full program should serve the purpose of evaluating the recruits and spotting other men with problems—then we can work on them privately."

"Now, you've hit my sore point," Kreins interjected. There's no way I can justify spending $1200 for this psychiatric program when we don't even have decent facilities or equipment—not enough lockers, no hot water, not even a camera. I'm not against this program, but I don't want to ask my men to take on a shrink—with all the ridicule that may come with it—unless they also have some chance to work in better surroundings than they have now."

"But this isn't an either-or situation," Wax responded. "If you need specific equipment, you come to Charlie Brown or me with a list, and we'll see that the essentials are taken care of somehow. But Ed is right, his program is already part of the standard procedure, and it's a separate budget item from anything else you may request. So let's talk about how to get that program started."

"Okay, if we get the things we need for the department, I'll go along with the program. But may I give you some advice?" he asked, turning to me. "I think I know police better than you do. . . ."

"Yes," I agreed.

"If you bring your whole package in, you'll get such resistance that it's going to fail. Why don't you begin with a lecture on some subject, then open it up for discussion. The men are used to going to school, so it won't be so different for them. Then see where it takes you."

The edge had gone out of Kreins's voice, and he seemed to genuinely care about getting this project off to a good start. And I agreed with him—a lecture with discussion wouldn't be too unusual for the men, and I could ease into the other aspects of the program after the men had become more accustomed to talking about themselves. In fact, talking about themselves and the self-examination that requires is the principal reason for the cops'—or anyone else's—suspicion or fear of me. They always claim to be content with themselves, though whether that's true is open for question. And this is what keeps them from accepting such a program—they don't want to be "open for question."

"That sounds good to me—I appreciate your suggestion. What's a good day for the first lecture?"

"Why not a week from today?"

"That fits into my schedule. I thought I'd talk about kids, particularly the rejected, runaway, rebellious sort who are around town so much these days."

"Fine," Kreins concluded, "I'll see that all the men are there."

The topic of kids seemed both appropriate and necessary in the fall of 1966. Sausalito was experiencing the first of the flower children, and as yet the city was not prepared for this phenomenon. The laws relating to juveniles were rather strict and inflexible: if a kid was camping out in a park or spending his days on the streets, the law specified that he be arrested for vagrancy and taken to juvenile hall. There were no "crash pads" or other special agencies for young people on their own—those came later, as social service groups responded to the burgeoning population of youngsters cut loose from their families.

Still, the police had some discretion in handling the kids. Both Huck, the former chief, and Kreins urged their officers to treat these young people with respect and concern, and Sausalito police were less eager to arrest or prosecute than to minimize drug use among the kids and to help anxious families get in touch with their children. This lenient attitude was not shared by police in other nearby communities, so Sausalito's street population grew as the word spread of this comparatively favorable treatment.

And the cops did try to handle the kids with restraint. But most officers could not understand what had made these young people leave their families and reject all the opportunities and material advantages their parents had offered. Many cops had a strong desire to help these young people, to rescue them from street life and its perils. But they found the kids hostile and seemingly unreachable. This, in turn, left the police frustrated and angry, and it ultimately diminished the good intentions of many officers.

My job in that first lecture was to help restore those good intentions—by giving the men some understanding of why the kids were so hostile and how they had acquired those attitudes. And before I met with the department I had to examine my own feelings to make sure that I wouldn't unconsciously project any of the old fear and mistrust I had felt toward police. I was already suspect in some cops' eyes, because of my profession and my liberal political views, and they'd soon find out that I was a Freudian to boot. Yet I was certain that my lecture—and the discussion I hoped would follow—could establish my "credentials" as a person who respects the police for the job they do and who wants to help them do it better.

The squad room was empty—of people, that is—when I arrived at 8:20 A.M., but it was cluttered with the paraphernalia of police work. Along one wall were twenty-four makeshift lockers—square wooden boxes that looked hastily built and slapped with a coat of dark stain. Until a week ago there had been no place for the men to store personal belongings. The other walls were papered with samplings from a seemingly endless stream of ink: WANTED posters, bulletins about training sessions and legal matters, maps of the city and county marked with various codes and flags, announcements of job openings in other departments. This room served as everything but holding cell—the men changed clothes here before and after their shifts; witnesses were interviewed here (at times other than between shifts); briefings were held here for officers going on duty. Now it would serve another purpose, as well, and I wondered how at least twenty men would arrange themselves among fourteen school desks in a windowless, fifteen-foot-square space.

My musings were interrupted by Chief Kreins, who boomed a good morning from the doorway. "All the men will be here except the five on duty now. I've told them it's a training lecture, but I don't think they know exactly what to expect. Actually, neither do I."

"We're all in the same boat there, because this is my first session with the whole department. I'll give my spiel, and then we'll play it by ear."

The men began to arrive, some in uniform, others in street clothes. I sat down at a desk that was up against the row of lockers, so that if there were any clowns in the group at least they couldn't get behind me and distract the others. Within a few moments all the desks were occupied, several men were standing, and a few more were seated on the floor with their backs propped against the wall. The chief rose to open the meeting, and as he stood I felt a quick wave of anxiety; it passed just as quickly, but I was aware that my collar was already damp with perspiration.

"Some of you have met Dr. Shev when he interviewed you, but for those who haven't, this is Dr. Edward Shev, a psychiatrist and neurologist who lives in Sausalito. Today he's going to talk to us about kids. Dr. Shev?"

"Thank you, Chief. I don't have to tell you men that

Sausalito has become the prime gathering place for dropped-out kids, runaway teenagers, alienated students, and a growing drug cult. What I'd like to talk about is how and why these kids are here."

"If you know. . . ." a low voice said. I ignored the voice and the stir it caused and kept talking. "There's an element in this situation that is just as important as the kids on our streets, but this is an unseen element—the parents." I introduced the concept of parental rejection, a phenomenon which precedes a child's casting off of his parents' values and life style. The parental rejection in most of these kids' lives consisted of giving the child everything he wanted, but without any discipline or real personal attention. This is the most sophisticated form of rejection—ignoring the child, saying to him, "Okay, you can do anything you want." That's just another way of saying, "We don't care what you do," or at least that's the message a child often gets from such "permissive" treatment. And by giving children such apparent freedom the parents are not really being permissive, they're being neglectful.

As background for this discussion I gave a brief summary of what I call the *triangle of life,* the basic Freudian interpretation of a child's relationship to his parents during his early, formative years. So far most of the men had listened quietly and—it seemed—attentively. Now one officer spoke: "Isn't the dynamics of development you're giving us pure Freud?" He didn't wait for an answer. "And isn't Freud pretty much out of the picture these days? How about giving us some theory by Reich?"

"You may think Freud is out of the picture, Sergeant; I don't. He pioneered the science of human behavior, and he's the whipping boy for everyone who came later. But if you want to discuss Reich, tell us what you know about him."

"Well," the sergeant paused briefly, "Reich says that sex can be good for something, instead of blaming everybody's faults on it, like Freud does."

"Not bad. But Freud doesn't so much *blame* sex for everybody's faults as much as he shows how stages of development are dependent on sexual maturity, don't you think? That's why I think a discussion like this is important: some kids are going to run away and get into trouble, and bring with them all sorts of problems from their background they may very easily transfer to *you*." I suggested that we postpone a discussion of Reich for another time, but I was glad the sergeant had brought it up. I wanted an atmosphere of challenge and debate that would help us all get a load off our chests so that we could penetrate to some of the more important—but rarely discussed—concerns of police. I finished my summary of children's development and asked for questions.

"Okay, Doctor, that helps me understand why these kids run out on their families, but how can I handle them when they're camped out on the sidewalk?"

Another officer answered for me. "I think what Dr. Shev is saying is that we can't treat these kids like we were their parents. And that's the way I feel toward them. So I'm going to have to kind of put myself in their shoes, treat them more like equals."

"That's right," I responded. "And you can insist on respect from them—for the police and for the laws that are necessary to make the city function. You just have to let the young people know that you expect cooperation. If that doesn't work—and there will always be some problems—you have the juvenile laws to enforce when the alternatives don't work."

"My approach is just to level with a kid who's gotten into trouble," a sergeant commented. "I tell him that society has certain rules and that I'm not in a position to say whether they're right or wrong, but my job is to enforce those rules. And if that youngster breaks the rules, he can expect punishment, which in my business usually means incarceration. That kind of talk seems to make a kid think about what he's gotten himself into."

"Yes, and it effectively removes you from the role of the enemy—the voice of authority—to a man who has a job to do. That's good."

"But Doc, what about a runaway juvenile? We don't really have much choice there; we have to call the kid's parents or take him to juvenile hall."

"Those are sort of narrow limits, but there is a suggestion you can give parents that I know has worked for some families. That is for the parents to tell their child that they're not going to make him a prisoner, they just want to talk over the problems they all have and see if they can find some answers. But if the youngster still feels that he can't stay at home with them, he is free to leave and they'll help him find a living situation that is what he feels he needs. Now, not all parents will be able to stomach this, but if they can and it's clear to the child that they mean it, then they have established a basis for communication."

"Don't some kids just run away or steal something so they'll be caught?" one officer asked.

"Let's hear some opinions on that."

"I think that's true—lots of kids know the policeman is there to do just that, to take them out of a bad situation. I had a boy who'd stolen a car; he was sent home from juvenile hall on probation, and he went right out and stole another car. His case worker told me this boy had a very violent stepfather and he felt he couldn't go back home. So he was sent to a detention center for a few months and then to a foster home. He's doing okay now."

By the end of the two-hour session most of the men had offered some personal comment or question, although they were all rather restrained. Yet this first lecture had confirmed my belief that most of the officers would be receptive to me, or at least give me a fair hearing. Only two men had refused to participate, except by offering barbs or whispering to others seated near them. The more persistent heckler—the one who'd mumbled "if you know" at the beginning—left before the meeting ended, purposely disrupting the discussion. (That man, in fact, remained hostile to me and my program for the several years he was a member of the Sausalito department.)

The other holdout was more reluctant than hostile. He was the oldest man on the force, a traditional tough Irish cop with thirty years' experience. During the discussion he took exception to a few of my points, suggesting that he had a lot more experience in these matters than I did, so why should he accept my theories? After the session—when everyone but the chief and I had left—this old-line cop cornered me with his own theory.

"Doc, I'll tell you how to handle kids. You've got to treat them fair, you've got to treat them square, you've got to tell them where you stand and where they ought to stand. And if they don't, you hit 'em in the ankles."

5

Discovering the Rescue Fantasy

I WOKE ABRUPTLY, sat up, and looked around. There wasn't a hint of light in the room. Something in my dream had interrupted my sleep, and I fought to bring its images back to my mind. The dream was about my family: my father had chastised me for some minor offense, and on this occasion my brother had joined in his criticism of me. I was accustomed to my father's ill temper, but I had always looked up to my brother for support—he had been a sort of surrogate parent to me. Now he was siding against me, and I felt hurt and resentful of this new attitude.

It seemed odd that I'd dream about my brother and father at this time; my father had been dead for many years and I hadn't spoken or corresponded with my brother in several months. As I tried to trace the origins of this dream, I realized that the feelings that had caused me to awaken—hurt and resentment toward a parent or surrogate parent—were often expressed by the police officers and applicants I had seen almost daily in recent weeks. My dream probably had been suggested by the men's accounts of troubled relationships with their parents or the absence of a parent and their ways of compensating for it.

In the morning I thought more about the dream, and I tried to recall how many times I'd heard someone describe an overtly or occultly broken home. Perhaps two-thirds of the almost 200 men I'd interviewed had discussed such circumstances, while some others had tried to cover up such situations. I felt that there might be a direct link between these men's family backgrounds and their own motivation to become police officers.

As I applied this idea to the basic dynamics of development, a conclusion became increasingly clear to me. By becoming police officers these men had chosen to work with people who've gotten into trouble—with the law or in their own lives (such as families whose violent quarrels result in neighbors' calling the police). The police are a bulwark of society, seeing that troubled people do not harm others or upset the established workings of the community. In a sense the cops are there to "rescue" society, and they quite literally rescue some of its members every day.

This concept fit perfectly with Freud's notion of a *rescue fantasy,*° which Jung and others later expanded to describe the motivation of people in the "helping professions"— ministers, doctors, social workers. The psychological literature contains numerous articles and case studies relating to the rescue fantasy, but no one had ever applied it to police. Yet a cop's work has the same basic purpose as that of doctors or ministers or social workers—to help people resolve their problems or in some way alleviate their pain. Now it seemed utterly simple: the police too were a helping profession, motivated by a fantasy of rescue.

The basis for this motivation is a person's relationship with his parents. In fact, every child experiences a simple form of

°A more detailed explanation of this theory will be found in the Appendix.

this rescue fantasy for a brief period, usually as a desire to possess the parent of the opposite sex. But in some parent-child relationships the signals are distorted: the child gets the message that he must actually "rescue" that parent, and this impulse to rescue will govern his choice of work as an adult.

Later that day I went over the notes I'd made during each screening interview. I found some evidence for my rescue fantasy theory in the file of almost every man I'd recommended for police work, as well as in my notes about many men who weren't recommended. The signs of their motivation were varied but always had to do with one parent's negative impact (or complete absence) and a resulting dependence on the child by the other parent. For example, a mother whose husband was a violent drunk had subtly or openly communicated to her son her need to be protected from the husband. The child's natural desire to possess and please his mother then became an urge to save her. The way each child handled the impulse to rescue his parent determined whether he matured as a sublimated personality, capable of independent thought and action, or a reactive one, still ruled by his desire to rescue and thus incapable of making decisions or taking action on his own. But the need to help, to rescue, remained the same—regardless of personality—in all of these police or would-be police.

I was excited about my discovery, and eager to gather more evidence to back it up. Of course the interviews would continue to give me this opportunity, but I wanted to get more feedback than they could provide. So I decided to introduce my rescue fantasy theory in a formal, detailed lecture—I would try it out on the police themselves.

The faces on the WANTED posters were different, but little else had changed in the squad room during my ten months of working with the Sausalito police. Now there were two more men on the force, an advantage at all times except in departmental meetings.

"Since it's a warm day I'll begin right away so that maybe we can finish a little early. Today I'm going to talk about the psychological motivation for police work, and some ideas I've developed as to why you are all here. You know, in the year that I've been meeting with you—or almost a year—we've covered lots of problems that police have to deal with, and in every discussion I've tried to help you understand what makes people act the way they do. Many of you have told me—and told the group on some occasions—that you've been able to relate better to people with problems—drunks, hostile kids, homosexuals, family quarrels—because you could begin to see their point of view. Now I'd like to see what you think about my analysis of why you're in this profession."

"I have two main themes today; one is the policeman's role in society and the other is the dynamics of behavior that make someone want to be a cop. First, let's talk about the role of a cop. I think we tend to forget what a policeman's job is in terms of the people he's dealing with. What kind of people are you dealing with?"

Officer: "The people we deal with most are the everyday citizens."

"Under what circumstances do you see them?"

Officer: "When they've done something wrong."

"Okay, when people are in trouble, how do they feel?"

Officer: "Pretty bad."

"They're anxious, aren't they? Now this is what you're dealing with—a tense person, and what does he expect from you?"

Officer: "Soothing. Help."

"What does that sort of make you?"

Officer: "A sucker? . . ." [Laughter.]

"Well, that's one thing. Do you know what a policeman is, really?"

Officer: "Some people call them pigs."

"Well, okay, they call me a head shrinker."

Officer: "That's good, too."

"I always have a good answer for that—I shrink heads down to their proper size.

"But back to the policeman. He's the same thing as any person in authority is. Those of you who've taken psychology, have you heard of a surrogate parent? Do you know what that term means? It's a symbolic substitute. And every policeman on the street has been designated by a citizen to be his surrogate parent, to be his conscience. The general public says, in effect, 'We've got a whole set of rules that we have to live by, to live with each other in an amicable manner. And what we need is a symbolic parent to supervise us.' That is the policeman—by virtue of our consent, you become our symbolic parent. And—this is very important—someone's reaction to a policeman is unconsciously going to be very much the way he related to his parents in the past. You remember Sam Levinson, school teacher who turned comedian? He used to get called and lined up with his seven brothers and sisters, and his father would go down the line and slap each of them. And he'd say, 'Dad, what did you do that for?' And his father would answer, 'If you don't know, you will later on in the day. That's just in case.' Well, you can imagine, if you're raised in this kind of atmosphere, how any kind of person in authority is going to make you feel.

"So a cop is there to help people, and he is given the role of surrogate parent by society. It's important for you—as police—to be aware of this and also to understand how you came to fill this role. Now, when I was beginning my screening interviews for this department, I felt that I needed to know more about the type of person who makes a good cop. So I interviewed fifty officers in San Francisco who were recommended by the chief there. In those interviews and many since then, I discovered that these men were saying the same things that we know that people who go into the ministry and medicine talk about. About 60 per cent of these men came from broken homes, and I found that another 30 per cent had 'covertly' broken homes—an ill parent, an alcoholic parent, or a passive parent. And doctors and ministers very often come from the same type of background as I found among these police. This interested me a great deal, because if what I was hearing from police was correct, I could make a comparison with the medical profession and could evaluate the reasons why these people wanted to be cops."

Sergeant: "Let me ask you a question."

"Go ahead."

Sergeant: "If you stopped fifty people on the street who were in this same age bracket, how would the percentages of broken homes and passive parents be?"

"This has been done for the general population; the percentage of broken homes runs about 32 per cent."

Sergeant: "Then this is substantially less than you find in police groups."

"Yes—or the medical group or the ministry group.

"Incidentally, a covertly broken home is far more hurtful than an overt one. A person can come to terms with divorce, establish relationships with his parents in their new roles. But in a covert broken home, the terms of those relationships are constantly changing, so the child can never quite get his bearings.

"What I've done in my evaluation is to take this information about policemen's backgrounds and analyze it according to the dynamics of human development, and I've come up with an explanation for why people become police. Now let me explain first that in terms of psychiatry, I'm basically a dynamicist; I believe that dynamic relationships produce emotional problems, and I've reduced this understanding down to my description of the triangle of life, which we discussed in our session on troubled kids."

I briefly reviewed the stages of a child's development, from infancy to puberty. The men were basically familiar with these ideas from their psychology courses and our previous discussions. As in my earlier lecture on parent-child relationships, I used examples that related to the police officers' work, so that they could readily see how psychological theory applies to their daily routine.

"You can understand why a child will be more apt to run away at the time of puberty—it's a rebellious situation, and the child needs to start to declare his independence. One problem with puberty in modern society is that we try to slow it down. It primitive societies, by the time the child reached puberty the parents had already arranged a marriage, and that child didn't live at home for more than a year or two of his puberty. Today, if you get out on your own by the time you're eighteen or nineteen, you're lucky. This is the modern lifestyle of our society; go to school, get more education, prepare for a career. And what does that do with normal psychological development? It hampers this development, suppresses it, makes it abnormal by causing a delay. And this has been the reason for a popular cry of the most recent generation: 'You must recognize that we're now able to perform sexually and give us the freedom for this, and we will assume the responsibility.' I don't know if this is right or wrong, but this is the way it begins. This is why the teenage child becomes such a difficult problem for public responsibility."

Officer: "Do kids realize all this?"

"Not really. They are somewhat aware, but only vaguely."

Sergeant: "So what's the problem—are the kids just growing up too fast for our society?"

"Well, our society hasn't accounted for the fact that they're growing up at a normal rate. See, we're trying to slow down on them."

Officer: "Why does the child finally stop being rebellious?"

"Because his great antagonism toward his father or mother, depending on which one it is, is attenuated by virtue of the fact that there is another boy or girl down the block who is enough like the father or mother to attract the young person's attention. The child's affection is displaced from the opposite parent to a peer, and suddenly the pressure is off the parents."

Officer: "What happens when you have a daughter and mother who dress alike?"

"You have to look to find out how much that mother is pushing the daughter to be like her. You may have a problem."

Officer: "Right down to the earrings."

"It sounds like the mother is trying to prevent that child from becoming an independent person."

Captain: "What about when the mother dresses like her daughter? Is she competing with her daughter?"

"She's trying to compete and suppressing her daughter by competing. A parent can do that much more easily than a child can do it to a parent."

Officer: "This is an age of disappointments, too, isn't it? Because the children go out and try to act like adults, and they don't succeed very often, and this sets up more rebellion against the parents."

"Absolutely. But remember we're confining ourselves to an ideal norm here. If the situation is not quite normal—say, the father drinks a bit, gets belligerent and yells at the mother, maybe hits her sometimes, the male child is caught up in a different set of circumstances. The mother may say to him, 'I can't stand to live with your father because of his behavior.' Then the boy may have an urge to take care of his mother and say to himself, 'Don't worry, when I grow up I'll take care of you.' So the fantasy gets stuck, like a broken record. The son thinks, 'I must rescue my mother from my father, because my father is abusive and causes my mother to be sick and I can do a better job of taking care of her.' In such an abnormal situation the rescue fantasy, as I call it, takes over from the normal sexual instinct.

"How many times have you picked up the newspaper and read about a child killing a parent who was abusing the other parent? That's the extreme of the rescue fantasy, the ultimate in rescuing a parent.

"But usually in relationships between parents there is an attitude of 'No matter how badly he treats me I'm going to stick with him—and it's none of your business.' The child gets this message, so the need to rescue is subdued into the unconscious, and it gets displaced outward, so that the person wants to help others. This can be done in a negative or a positive way. By positive, I mean when the person reaches puberty he is mature enough to say to himself, 'There's nothing I can do about my mother and father's situation. They just sort of deserve one another, and I don't have to be part of it.' And all the anger and hatred that a person has built up against this relationship and the self-pity that he has imposed on himself gradually gets resolved. But the nagging theme of rescuing the mother remains, so he seeks jobs that will help other people. Now why one goes into medicine, ministry, teaching, and so forth is dependent on a number of factors—the degree of the relationship with the parents and its effect on the child, family tradition, economic and intellectual status, and so forth."

The room was very quiet now; no one was whispering or trying to get his paper work done during the lecture. The men's faces were intent—some looked skeptical, some thoughtful, a few seemed to show agreement or recognition of my comments as perhaps valid for their own experience. I knew the barrage of questions wasn't far off, though, so I took advantage of the attention while I had it. And I turned the analogy directly toward the men.

"I believe that these same dynamics of motivation apply to police—all of you are in some way governed by the rescue fantasy in your own backgrounds. Now, if you have in effect resolved all of these feelings—again ideally—then your motivational need to help people can be satisfied. By that I mean that if you help somebody out of trouble, you'll get an internal gratification from helping that person. It's not a matter of money or thanks or anything else, just internal gratification at what you've been able to do.

"Okay. If this gets integrated into your ego personality, then when you handle the displaced relationships that you encounter in your type of work, you'll do it with as gentle, firm, warm an understanding as one human being can give another. You're not angry at anybody, even though you're seeing a reenactment of your own childhood situation. But you do feel that you want to help people in trouble. And as police you deal almost exclusively with people in trouble, people who are looking for help.

"And the way you help them is dependent upon how you've resolved your own situation. If your father was an alcoholic and very abusive to your mother, and you come upon such a situation in your work, you may 'rescue' that drunk in a negative way. You'll help him, all right, but as you help him you may hit him an extra couple of times, just to get even with the old man, whom you couldn't hit when you were small. That's the way you might handle it if you hadn't resolved the need to rescue a parent from the other parent.

"Now, this is all unconscious, all something that motivates a person to respond to a stimulus on an unconscious level. You may feel these unconscious feelings and check them by countering them. You know you're going to react a certain way, so you protect yourself by being overcautious, overgentle—and in a sense, uptight—about what you're doing, so that you don't let go of your feelings. When you respond this way, then you're not in an integrated state, you're in a reactive state, because you are reacting to a stimulus in a counterresponse."

Officer: "Maybe I missed your point, but it seems like

Discovering the Rescue Fantasy / 91

you're saying that we're all from broken homes or we all had one or both parents who were alcoholics—and I don't think all policemen are that way, at least not the ones I know. And it's not true in my case."

"Well, you've had some kind of situation in the home to generate this motivation, something you may not recognize yourself. For instance, if one parent in the home is continually ill and there is a great need for care, then the child's whole orientation may be to get the mother's or father's love by taking care of that parent, to nurse him or her. In other cases it can be much more subtle—there's nothing wrong with either parent on a visible level, but the child knows deep down that one parent just isn't *there* when needed by the other, and I mean isn't there in the sense that the parent is just too passive or doesn't seem to care or can't be depended upon to assume responsibility in the family. This can have a very deep impact on the child.

"Now, to get back to your role: since you are a surrogate parent to the public, how you relate to citizens will reflect how you remember the way your parents treated you."

Sergeant: "But how could someone relate well to the public if he grew up with such an awful home life?"

"Here's where our own surrogate parents come in—an aunt or uncle, minister, teacher, or coach—someone to whom we have displaced our feelings about parents, in effect saying, 'these are the people I will identify with; they are the good parents.'"

Officer: "I get from your theory that every time a person meets another with superior knowledge and a superior position, that person is a surrogate parent. Is this true?"

"That's more or less true."

Officer: "Well, then, when you go to a clothing store and talk to the salesman, who has superior knowledge of what's in the store, is he a surrogate parent?"

"Yes. When you stop to think about it, you may say to him, 'Do you think this collar looks good on me?' It takes you back to the same situation as when you were a child and your parents took you to a store and told you what clothes looked good on you. In that moment the salesman becomes a surrogate parent—they're all around us."

Captain: "What is the difference between the peer group and surrogate parents? Don't people confide in friends and use them for the same sort of help?"

"Yes—sometimes there is no difference. Some people use peer relationships as displaced parental relationships. Remember I said earlier that as children we go through a phase of reinforcement of identification, when we use our peers to test out our sexual identity and our relationships with our parents. And as adults people often do this, too. Siblings also can affect this."

Officer: "When you talk with someone, like the interviews you did with recruits and some others here, can you pick out things about our family background even if we don't say them? Are the symptoms that apparent?"

"To the trained eye and ear, yes. If you could analyze just a moment's conversation—put it in a computer, say, and sort of stand aside and see what's going on subconsciously even as you're talking—you'd discover a lot of things going on that you were not aware of about yourself. And this is really the advantage a psychiatrist has—he spends fifteen years enlarging upon all kinds of contacts and relationships that he hears about and experiences. And he relates them to a scheme of behavior—learned in his training—in almost an instantaneous way.

"It's the same process you go through as police officers, combining your training with your gut reactions to each situation. Most of the time you can't stop and think about how you're going to act—you just do it. And that's why I want to help you become aware of what factors from your background and experience are affecting the way you respond or make decisions today."

No one else asked a question, so I adjourned the meeting.

Discovering the Rescue Fantasy / 93

But no one left the room right away, either. The men began talking among themselves, and several of them came forward to relate personal comments that they apparently weren't ready to share with the group. I felt that I'd really connected in this session; I'd given the men familiar psychological information and then applied my interpretation directly to them. And they had been receptive, if a bit skeptical. (In fact, if they hadn't been skeptical, I'd have known they weren't really listening.) The new ideas seemed to have struck home for these cops—an important beginning. Yet there was a long way to go from the glimmer of recognition today to what I hoped to see eventually—police whose self-knowledge and self-esteem make them the best cops they could be.

6
Coming to Grips with "Society's Garbagemen"

ONE EVENING I passed a police car as I pulled into my carport. The officer was a man I'd screened a month before, and when he recognized me he backed up opposite my drive. He asked if I had a moment to talk and, when I nodded, he began his story.

"There's a waitress at the restaurant where I usually go for coffee who seems to hate me, and I can't figure out why. I just transferred here, so she can't have a grudge against me and I know I've never met her. But she's really hostile when I come in, takes her time about waiting on me, and today she shoved the coffee at me so it spilled, and I'm sure it was on purpose."

What may have sounded like a petty complaint was, I knew, actually an important step forward. For the past several months many of the officers had stopped by my house on their way to and from patrol, to discuss specific problems they wanted to work on immediately. As in this case with the waitress, the matter would be seemingly insignificant, but combined with other problems it could mushroom daily and bring intolerable pressures to bear on a cop's life. And I knew that this officer had taken the first crucial step: he could not let the situation simmer until it finally boiled over—he had to act.

I observed that it sounded like the waitress was trying to provoke him, perhaps because she'd had some bad experience with police in the past.

"Yeah, she makes cracks about me to other customers, too—just loud enough for me to hear. So far I haven't said anything to her. How should I handle this, Doc?"

"My suggestion is that you say to her, 'May I ask you a question?'—then ask why she's trying to provoke you."

The officer frowned, and said, "You mean I should come right out and accuse her?"

"You're just stating a fact."

"Well . . . isn't it more of an opinion?"

"I doubt it, but even if it is, you'll know by her reaction if you're right."

"What do you mean? What kind of reaction should I expect?"

"I can't say exactly—I don't even know the woman. And besides, I don't want to spoil your fun, so to speak. What I'm really saying is that you should bring the situation out in the open."

"Well, I don't know," he mused, starting the squad car's engine, "but I guess I'll give it a try."

About ten days later I was in the squad room for our monthly bull session. These were informal, voluntary meetings that attracted a core of interested participants and a varying number of less involved members. I had purposely scheduled these sessions to coincide with the shift change, because it allowed men both going on and coming off duty to take part, and yet the general level of activity made it easy for someone to consult me or ignore me without being conspicuous.

One man clearly wasn't worried about being conspicuous, though—he hailed me the moment he entered the room:

"Hey, Doc, it worked!" It was the officer who'd stopped at my house the week before. His enthusiastic greeting got everyone's attention, so I asked if he'd explain the situation to the group.

He repeated his experience with the waitress, adding a few more details for this larger audience. "I walked in and sat down, then motioned for that waitress to come over before she had a chance to ignore me. I said, 'Can I ask you a question?' and she sort of curled her lip and said 'Okay.' So I said, 'Why do you always try to provoke me?' And she just opened her mouth, turned real red, and looked flustered. She stuttered around for a couple of seconds, then she said, 'I'm not trying to provoke you,' and put her order book up in front of her face and asked if I wanted anything besides coffee. That was a week ago, and ever since she's been as sweet as can be."

"Why do you think it worked?"

"I guess I embarrassed her into being decent."

"Sort of—but you did make her realize how she was behaving without being hostile yourself."

"Are you saying we should sort of turn the other cheek?" one sergeant asked.

Chief Kreins, who'd joined the group in time to hear about the waitress, answered this query. "Well, I wouldn't put it quite that way, because that implies maybe we're not willing to be tough when we have to. But I think this is a good example of the kind of police-community relations we could have most of the time—being courteous, but making citizens face up to their actions. That's the major part of law enforcement, and most often we deal with people whose actions have gone against the law. But I believe that we'll get more respect from the public if we try to meet them on a human level, like Scotty's confronting the waitress with the way she was treating him."

Lightning didn't flash in the room, or anything similarly

spectacular, but the nodding heads and mumbled agreement showed that these men understood the chief's point. It was a moment of recognition for me, too: I felt that my lectures and bull sessions had begun to pay off, for the men were learning to think in terms of human behavior as well as police procedure when doing their jobs.

Another officer's comments confirmed that feeling for me. He reported that one night during his routine patrol along the waterfront he happened to fall in behind a car being driven by a middle-aged black man. Both cars took the same route for several minutes, moving slowly among the industrial buildings and piers, until the car in front suddenly stopped. The driver jumped out and strode back to the police car, which had also halted abruptly.

"Why are you following me?" the man demanded angrily. "Can't a black person do anything around here without being harassed and treated like a criminal?"

"While he was raving at me for tailing him," the officer explained, "I realized that my regular patrol had a whole different meaning for this man. Maybe he'd been in trouble in the past—certainly he'd been hassled; it sort of goes with the territory of being black in a rich white city. So I let him finish and then said in as offhand a way as I could, 'Do you think I have nothing better to do than follow you? Why are you being so paranoid?' I added that I hadn't been following him but just happened to be going in the same direction and he'd gotten there ahead of me. For a minute he didn't seem to believe me—it was like he wanted to stay mad—but he gradually calmed down and muttered something about looking for boxes because he was moving. Well, I said, 'fine, good luck,' and backed up to pull around his car and finish my patrol."

The officer turned to me. "You know, Doc, a year ago—before we started these sessions—I wouldn't have taken that kind of abuse from anybody. I'd have gotten just as angry as he was and cited him for unsafe driving or mouthing off to a peace officer or something. But holding my temper brought some benefits this time. That guy changed his attitude toward police and he even called to give me a tip about two weeks later. He didn't know my name, but he described me and said I patrolled the waterfront, and the dispatcher got him through to me. He told me about some teenage kids who were robbing homes and autos, and he told me where they hid their stolen goods. He was right, too—we watched the place and broke up a small theft ring."

The men were impressed—it was the first time most of them had heard about the source of this tip. I told the man that he'd handled the situation well and thanked him for giving the psychiatric program some credit for his success. Then I asked if anyone else could report a similar experience, and was greeted with a conspicuous silence. Finally one sergeant offered, "No, Doc, but I get a lot of complaints."

More silence.

"What's the matter, have you guys suddenly gotten self-conscious? As I recall from our past sessions, you can't wait to talk about your run-ins or exploits."

The sergeant who'd raised the topic of complaints spoke up. "All I know is, if it ever gets to the point where you have to sacrifice your safety—or somebody else's—'cause you're worried about complaints, you better get another job."

Another officer joined in. "Yeah, we had a perfect example of that the other night. The manager of a supermarket called, said a customer had told him there was a man with a gun parked outside the store. It was closing time, and he wanted us over there in a hurry to prevent a robbery. He said the customer was reliable and wouldn't make it up, and he had seen the car himself. So two of us hustled over, spotted the car, and I approached with my gun drawn while Al covered me. I had the man get out, spread him, and checked for a weapon, but found nothing. I wasn't rough, but I'm sure I intimidated the guy, and he was pretty shook up. Turns out his wife worked in a restaurant across the street—he was waiting for her. I apologized for the show of force and mentioned the call we'd had, then we left.

"Now that guy could come in here and complain, but we went according to straight procedure, on the assumption that there was a gun. We couldn't afford to discount the source of that tip or worry about what he might do if we rousted him for no reason. We weren't about to get shot just for being nice."

"What else could you have done?" another man asked.

"That's what I'm saying—nothing else. But what's bad is if the department is set up so that nobody listens to complaints. Then this guy could raise hell, maybe take it to court. But if you have a system of 'the sympathetic ear,' you can avoid those kinds of problems, at least most times."

"And you've got to recognize, too," I put in, "that this person has a perfectly valid complaint from his point of view. You might tell him you realize that."

The way cops say things, the way they handle volatile situations, the way they control their own temper, the way they regard the people they come in contact with—all of these things come out in a bull session like this, and all of them have indirect but significant bearing on how a cop handles himself in day-to-day situations. At this point we were involved with the immediacy of events that occur when the men are on patrol. Soon the talk turned to the root of some complaints—the men's attitudes toward citizens and the public's feelings about cops. One man summarized it this way: "Cops are here to stay, and people realize that. As long as you don't mess with them, they won't mess with you."

"Sounds simple, but what does that mean?" I asked him.

"It means that the general public doesn't give a damn about the police."

"I think the police are the last stronghold keeping society

together," another officer stated. "We're the only ones who will handle any situations of violence or potential violence. The schools, the social agencies, nobody else wants to handle violence calls. We're out there doing our jobs—and yet we know the guy we arrest will be back on the street in an hour. We're not giving up, even though the courts and the government are so fouled up they can't do their jobs."

A low voice said, "I feel like we ought to clap."

"Society's garbagemen, huh?" I said when the laughing died down.

Someone else agreed: "That's a good way to put it. We're the only ones keeping the wolf away from the door. But I think the cop's giving up."

"Have you given up?" I asked.

"I didn't say I'm giving up; I haven't given up yet. But let me tell you something, Doc—it gets harder every day to put the uniform on and come to work."

"Why?"

"Because you don't get the support from the public, that's why. I'm out there doing a job and I have to put up with all the crap that they don't want to put up with. And yet when you ask for something or you put your heart on your sleeve for them, all they want to do is come in and complain about you. 'This guy called me "Buster," ' or 'This guy did this . . . .' "

"I didn't think they used that term 'Buster' any more."

"It's not my term, Doc. [Laughter.] I'm just telling you what happens. I'm not saying it's right."

The men shared a few more incidents, then they moved on to the day's business. The session had served its purpose of letting the men blow off steam, share their gripes, and laugh at themselves. By learning that equally capricious or ironic things happen to each of them, these cops could get a healthier perspective on themselves and their work. And police with such a perspective are less likely to start

Coming to Grips With "Society's Garbagemen" / 101

believing that people are "out to get them" or something similar, and in turn they are less likely to react to the public as a collection of criminals or disgruntled taxpayers who want to make the cop's life miserable.

Yet some of the problems the men aired at bull sessions were too complex for group conversation. The men knew that I was available for individual counseling, and several of them had seen me privately. But I felt that I could help them solve specific problems in their work if I could observe them on the job. So, with the chief's approval, I began riding with the police on patrol. This new component of the program gave me a closer look at both the men and their work, which had some immediate results.

For the first time I had an opportunity to evaluate my earlier conclusions about the candidates I'd screened; now these men were functioning police and I could measure their performance against my expectations. (Generally my estimation of a candidate's potential proved true, partly because I had become pretty proficient at interviewing people for police work and partly because the chief and training officers in Sausalito were competent professionals.) And riding with the men on patrol also let me observe the cops who had never been screened. Some of these men had emotional hang-ups that affected their work—one or two probably shouldn't have been cops at all. But by seeing them in routine working situations, I could spot specific problems—usually involving their attitudes toward citizens—and later give them examples of those problems. I knew that some of the officers who needed counseling the most would be most resistant to my help, but I could get around that hurdle during lectures or bull sessions by discussing "hypothetical" incidents that might hit home with these cops.

For instance, handling alcoholics is a source of trouble for many police. Because many of these men have felt the devastating effects of alcoholism in their own families, the old hang-ups return when they confront someone whose drinking is the cause for police action. Many cops' emotional reaction to such situations can only be resolved through intensive counseling, but for purposes of their work the men are able to take a sort of shortcut: so long as a cop recognizes his hang-up, he can keep his emotions in check by responding in an opposite way to his impulsive reaction. In other words, the officer could subdue his urge to punch a drunk in the nose and also consciously try to counteract the emotions that triggered that impulse, perhaps by saying to himself— "This man is not my father; I'm here to help everyone in this situation, and I can't be effective if I'm angry." When we discuss such examples at a mandatory departmental meeting, something is bound to rub off on even the most recalcitrant men.

More often, though, the Sausalito police were receptive to my questions and suggestions. One man, Patrolman Jordan, asked that I ride with him, because he seemed to spend an inordinate amount of time in court defending the traffic tickets he had handed out. In fact, the rate that motorists challenged this man's tickets was five times that of the department's average—about 20 per cent of his citations were disputed, compared with 4 per cent for the rest of the force.

The reason was not hard to spot. While I was riding with him, Jordan saw the car ahead make an illegal left turn. He made the same turn himself, hit the flashing light and gave a short blast of the siren. The motorist pulled over, and the cop marched up to him with one hand over his pistol as the other hand drew the ticket book from a side pocket. The driver saw this, of course, and his look of confused apology turned to set-jawed defiance. Jordan's expression was similarly unyielding, and they both went away mad after a terse exchange. "That's one fellow I'll probably see in court," the officer said when he got back in the car.

Coming to Grips With "Society's Garbagemen" / 103

I asked if he had any idea why, and the officer replied that the driver had been hostile and resistant right off the bat. In response to my other questions he said he didn't think *he'd* caused the driver's attitude and that by being short with the man he'd just given him "a taste of his own medicine."

Then I asked Jordan to describe exactly how he had walked from the squad car to the citizen's car. He couldn't.

"What were you thinking at that moment?"

"I was thinking how could this guy with a local parking sticker on his rear bumper be so stupid or so arrogant as to make that turn right in front of me?"

"It never occurred to you that the driver might have made an honest mistake?"

"No—how could he? He *lives* here."

This was one time when a movie camera would've worked wonders, but I was limited to words and gestures, so I made the most of it. I told the officer that we'd do a brief episode of role-playing—he was to be the motorist, I was to be the cop. For dramatic purposes I borrowed his holster and ticket book. He watched as I walked casually up the street a few yards, then turned toward him with a menacing look and obviously put my hand over the gun, poised for action. I brandished a fistful of tickets in my other hand, stalking the squad car as if it contained three or four of the Ten Most Wanted.

He was genuinely surprised: "You mean I look like that?" I just nodded, then walked around to the passenger's door. He got out of the car to replace his gun belt and stood with his back to the car for a full minute. Then he mused, "Well, I guess I see why that guy was so hostile—you mean it was my attitude he was picking up, not the other way around."

For the next two hours we talked about laws and their importance, which offenses are the real threats to society and which aren't, and so on. I left him with suggestions on how to make a quick assessment of every infraction he witnessed, and how to coach himself on the relative unimportance of such things as an illegal left turn. I also left a more thoughtful and considerate man than I'd joined that morning.

The event pointed out the importance of the police-psychiatrist relationship. Jordan had been through a police academy and departmental training, plus side-by-side coaching by a senior officer, and yet he still displayed the kind of provocative attitude that could eventually ruin his career. But Jordan was not a bad cop, he simply needed professional advice from someone other than his peers or superiors. Who could better explain the psychological impact of his actions, after all, than a psychiatrist who had worked with him before?

That morning was almost a year to the day from my first lecture to the Sausalito department. During that time I had instituted all my original plans for the program—lectures, bull sessions, individual counseling—and the new component of riding with police on patrol had been added. This psychiatric in-service program had grown almost organically, with each new element added as the men's needs required it, and as they were ready to participate and benefit from it. (Today most departments depend only on psychological screening tests, which, from my vantage point, are only a small part of what must become a multidimensional psychiatric support program for *all* police departments.)

A few weeks later I added one more component to the program, this one based on the needs of both the men and their wives. I had seen the benefits of bull sessions for the men—sharing gripes, blowing off steam, asking questions about human behavior—and I was sure that group meetings would also be helpful to the policemen's wives, who must share many of their husbands' emotional burdens and who have some special problems because they are married to cops. The women couldn't be required to attend a lecture, though, and I didn't know how many of them would want to participate. At the next departmental lecture I posted a

Coming to Grips With "Society's Garbagemen" / 105

notice of my first open session for wives, and the men were enthusiastic about the idea.

I needn't have worried. Several women were there when I arrived at the bank's meeting room (the squad room was too busy and distracting and not private enough for this session), and the room filled quickly. I opened with the observation that I hadn't been certain whether the women would come. One wife's response set things straight: "After hearing about you for a year, did you think we were going to miss this?"

Nor should I have doubted their desire to participate in such a meeting. In fact, the discussion became more open and personal—more quickly—than with any group of men I'd seen. The initial concern these wives expressed was for their husbands' work; they wanted my perspective of where they fit in. The police wives recognized that their husbands were in a dangerous job—and for the most part they had accepted this. Several members of the group told of asking their husbands to consider changing to some other type of work, but they all knew beforehand what the response would be. *Why* he wouldn't change jobs, however, was another matter entirely, and as I led a discussion on the special motivations that lead people into police work, I felt that the women were beginning to understand their husbands' roles as cops more completely than they ever had before. We would eventually go into the rescue fantasy in depth, but for now I also wanted to touch upon a very important area of concern for all police wives.

That concern was the special problems that go with being a cop's wife, especially the way she is treated because of her association with law enforcement. One woman posed the problem well: "I feel that we have different problems than other families do. Our husbands' lives are put on the line, and we have to live with that. Then we may meet a person who tells of a bad incident with a police officer, and naturally we take a defensive attitude. And our children have it, too—other kids tell them their father's a pig. When I'm in a situation like that I say, 'Not all cops are bad,' but it usually doesn't change anything."

Another woman told of a more positive experience. She and her husband and children entertained a group of students from the University of California at Berkeley for a day. None of the guests knew that their host was a policeman, and when the dinner conversation turned to the subject of cops, the family didn't clue in the students. Later the husband left for work and someone asked his occupation; they were amazed and embarrassed to learn that he was one of the "pigs" they had been deriding. But the experience transformed the students' attitudes: "We have letters from each of them saying how seeing our family had changed their view of cops."

Another wife asked how to resolve conflicting pressures on children, particularly teenagers whose peers encourage them to try drugs or disregard certain other laws. I replied that there are many ways to approach this, but basically the parents are role models for their children. "If you and your husband handle his role with dignity—if it is clear that you respect each other and he has respect for himself in his work—then the children will get that message."

Another woman returned to the problem of public hostility toward police and their families. "One thing that bothers me is that it's very difficult to get it across to people that policemen are governed by laws, which they have to follow in their work. And I think too many people blame the police for the *laws.*"

"They've got to displace their anger onto someone," I observed.

"Yes, but it doesn't belong there."

"You and I know that, but the public. . . ."

"Somebody please tell them!"

Coming to Grips With "Society's Garbagemen" / 107

"Who do you think could tell them?"

"The newspapers, television commentators. Those kinds of people."

"And even then, do you think people would listen? Do you think it would make any difference the next time your husband gives a speeding ticket or stops a drunk on the street?"

The room was silent.

"Well, what are you saying," someone finally answered, "that we should just give up on trying to educate the public?"

"No, I think we—all of us—should always keep trying to explain the cop's role and why it is needed. But I'm also saying that we should simply accept the fact that most people will never understand."

"I think that's true. Even our closest family friends make remarks that to me are really unkind."

"Like what?"

"Oh, they joke about the pig image or they make references to beating up people as if that's what cops do all the time."

"How do you respond to this?"

"Well, we just laugh it off, I guess, rather than start an argument."

"Maybe you should start an argument."

Another woman spoke. "At our house we do neither. If the time is right to talk about cops and their role these days, we talk about it. But these constant references or little jokes or barbs aren't worth bothering with. We decided a long time ago to rise above it and get on with something else."

A woman in the back said, "Right. I think you have to develop a team effort. It's like Dr. Shev says, the public isn't going to change its opinion of police for a long time. So meanwhile you might as well bolster up the family instead."

"What do you mean by that?"

"Well, I mean that our kids are aware that what their father does isn't always too popular with lots of people. So sometimes they're going to hear remarks about cops from other kids, but it doesn't mean anything because *we* know at home that what he does is good, and we're proud of him."

"You mean you tell your kids to *expect* trouble?" a younger woman asked.

"Sure. We also let them hear about his day when we sit down to dinner. It's come to be a kind of regular event. He doesn't talk about some of the rougher stuff, and in fact it's the little things they enjoy most. He can make the problem of getting a cat out of a tree so hysterically funny, they just love it. And I think it's really brought us closer."

"I don't know," said the younger woman. "You try to raise your kids in a normal environment and not make them have to cope with your own troubles."

"Well, let's talk about this idea of a normal environment," I said, moving into a discussion of the difference between security and normalcy, the kinds of ties that make a family close, and the ways a cop can best share his work with his wife and kids. Throughout that session and in subsequent meetings, I felt a growing respect for these women. They confronted and explored problems with greater depth and candor than many of their husbands did in small group sessions, and they were especially mature in discussing more painful subjects, such as impotence and homosexuality, that in many cases were simply never discussed at home. It took time, many group sessions, and sometimes individual counseling to break some of these barriers down.

It struck me then, as it has many times after group sessions with the men, what extraordinary pressures we as a society expect our police officers and their families to handle—and how little help we give them. Without some kind of consistent, on-the-spot psychiatric counseling program that is geared to deal with *all* phases of the cop's life, how can we

Coming to Grips With "Society's Garbagemen" /

expect these men and women to maintain stable, objective, and professional attitudes in their work day after day? Especially when we consider that nearly one-third of all cops are unsuitable for police work and should never have been hired in the first place, the need for psychiatrists within police departments grows ever more urgent.

7
The Program Works for One Man

DAVE MALKIN was an unknown quantity. He'd been hired as a sergeant by Chief Kreins, one of five men taken on without my screening or even being consulted. Of course he'd been in my in-service program for two years, not at all hostile but not enthusiastic, either. As a cop and supervisor he seemed competent—at least I hadn't heard of any complaints from his subordinates or from citizens. My impression was that he was basically a sound officer, but I had no real knowledge of him as a person.

So I was interested to learn how he handled a tense—and potentially deadly—situation in Sausalito one Saturday. One of the four men on duty that night, Sergeant Malkin was in charge of the 4 P.M.-to-midnight shift. He gave a short briefing to remind the officers which vacationing residents' homes should be checked and to alert them to revisions of arrest procedures. Then the three men went on patrol, each in his own squad car, and the sergeant remained at the station as watch commander.

At 5 P.M. Malkin got a call from Officer Terry, one of the three men on patrol, who reported hearing gunfire in the vicinity of Wolfback Ridge. This is an area of steep, rugged slopes high above the residential streets of Sausalito. It is lonely and isolated, dotted with several abandoned rock quarries—the ideal place for kids with BB guns or someone taking more serious target practice.

Malkin instructed the officer to walk to a point above the area where he could see down into the quarry from which the shots seemed to be coming, then to report back. In the meantime he radioed the Highway Patrol and the county sheriff's office to ask that they seal off all possible exits from the ridge. The city boundaries were such that although the shots were coming from Sausalito, if the people firing them fled they would be out of that jurisdiction within seconds. Malkin described this situation very carefully to the other departments' dispatchers; he didn't want to alarm anyone, least of all the people with the weapons.

Within five minutes Officer Terry called in. He'd crawled to the edge of a cliff above the quarry and had seen what looked like target practice—three men firing automatic rifles at human-shaped targets, with two women standing by. They appeared to be part of some radical group; all wore military-style clothing and two of the men had ammunition belts over their shoulders. Their car was parked on a fire road at the edge of the quarry; the hood was covered with boxes of ammunition and several pistols. Malkin told Terry to stay there, but out of sight and close to his car—he'd receive further instructions within a few minutes. The sergeant then called the other two officers on patrol (they had heard Terry's reports on their radios) and advised them to meet him on Alta Road, below the quarry, in five minutes. Malkin took another squad car and drove toward the top of the ridge where Terry waited. He checked with the sheriff's and Highway Patrol's dispatchers and determined that one car with two officers was blocking each possible escape route, out of sight of the five people in the quarry.

Now Malkin had a choice to make. He was in charge; his actions could defuse the impending confrontation, or the police presence might spark an explosive shootout. He was aware that several politically militant groups were active in the county and that some of their members advocated violence and condemned the "police state." He also knew the law—firing of any weapon was prohibited within Sausalito's city limits—and he knew he'd have to arrest these people. The question was how.

The most obvious option was to follow straight police procedure, as defined in textbooks and taught in police academies. In this instance it would mean assembling all available officers, surrounding the area, then calling for the "suspects" to put down their weapons and come out (yes, just like on television). That approach could be called "tough but legal."

Malkin might also have taken a very tough and questionably legal course. This would be the maximum show of force: police with rifles and shotguns aimed down into the quarry from all sides, a hasty command for the suspects to drop their weapons, perhaps the order for the police to fire if the suspects didn't disarm quickly enough or if they took cover behind the quarry's man-sized boulders. Such actions would be based on standard police procedure, but could easily result in the worst kind of stalemate: hostile, trigger-happy cops exchanging bullets with paranoid, militant citizens. On bone-dry Wolfback Ridge that would almost certainly mean a fire that could threaten half the homes in Sausalito, in addition to whatever death or injury it caused.

But Malkin also had a third option. He could choose to disregard the standard procedure, or at least the parts of it he thought might inflame the situation. His responsibility was to stop the shooting, without endangering the residents or police, and to arrest the suspects.

By the time he reached Terry's position on the ridgetop,

Malkin had made his choice. He would depart from the standard show of force and make it clear to the five people in the quarry that the police meant business but weren't going to come out shooting. He motioned for Terry to follow him, and both cars circled down to Alta, just as the other two officers arrived. Malkin knew that the cars could be seen from the quarry above now, and as he looked up two armed men stepped into his line of vision.

The four officers assembled on the downhill side of their parked cars, and Malkin gave his instructions: "Bradshaw and Spencer, when we leave, you get your shotguns but keep them out of sight behind the cars. Terry and I are going up there." Malkin turned to Terry: "We'll keep our guns holstered and just walk up that path as casually as we can, like this is no big deal and those men up there aren't holding M-1's or something."

"Okay," came the somewhat hesitant reply.

Malkin led the way up the rocky, rather steep path. They were in full view of the people above; and there was no cover, had the officers wanted to hide. Both men were out of breath by the time they neared the crest of the hill. That fact may have made the two policemen less threatening and more human; Malkin's greeting certainly did. "Whew! That's quite a hill."

The two men standing at the edge of the hill shifted positions, their guns held at their sides and pointed toward the ground. Now, face-to-face with the cops, they weren't hostile or menacing—they were just self-conscious. Their companions huddled in the background, apparently trying to shield the ammunition and other guns from view.

"Guess you know why we're here," the sergeant offered. "It's against city ordinance to discharge firearms within the city limits."

Nobody moved. The men said nothing.

"We're going to have to confiscate your weapons and take you down to the station," Malkin continued.

Still no word or movement from the two men.

"Could we have those rifles, please?" Malkin stepped forward toward one man, reaching out his left hand. Terry followed suit, facing the other man. Another few moments passed, then both rifles rose in unison and changed hands.

"You know you have the right to remain silent . . ." Malkin began.

"Yeah, we've been through that before."

Terry moved toward the other three people, who stepped aside and let him retrieve the pistols and remaining rifle from the car's hood. Then the officer patted down each suspect, first explaining that this was part of his job. Malkin stepped to the edge of the hill, holding both rifles, and motioned for the other two police to come up. Terry checked the inside of the car for weapons but found none, and so began transferring the firearms and ammunition to the edge of the hill. Bradshaw collected the targets. Then the four officers—each carrying guns or ammunition—escorted their five "prisoners" down the slope. There had been no need for handcuffs, tough talk, shots, or even drawn service revolvers. There was no need for talk now, save a curse when an off-balance policeman slipped on the rocky path.

The five men and women were driven to the station in two cars and taken inside. Malkin directed that the three men be booked and held, but he said the two women could go because they had not been observed holding or firing weapons. One of the women called a lawyer, and by six-thirty the men were out on bail. Malkin knew that these people were wise enough not to use that quarry for target practice any more; he hoped they had also learned something about the Sausalito police.

I heard about this episode a few days after it happened, and at the next bull session I asked Malkin if he'd make an appointment to discuss it with me. He seemed surprised, asking if he'd done something wrong. I assured him that the opposite was true—I wanted to interview him because his

handling of the target practice incident had been so successful.

During our discussion he confirmed what I had suspected:
he "was taking a tactical approach" and "trying to ease the
situation by being casual." He pointed out something many
cops would have lost sight of when faced with people firing
automatic rifles at human-shaped targets—that this was a
minor infraction, despite the frightening implications of the
scene. And he was aware from the moment Officer Terry
reported hearing gunfire that this situation—like so much of
police work—called for a series of judgments as well as
actions. Dave Malkin had made the right judgments—but not
necessarily the right ones by the book—and they had paid off.

"The bonus came," Malkin told me, "when one of three
men said he had never been treated so courteously by any
cop, anywhere. And that came from a guy who was probably
thinking of me as a target an hour before."

Malkin enjoyed that bonus, even though it was a sort of
left-handed compliment. But he didn't do it for the praise,
nor does any policeman do his job in anticipation of rewards
or compliments. The basic characteristic of a cop's motivation is satisfaction from doing the work, from helping
people, although different police use different methods to
get the job done. On that Saturday night in Sausalito Dave
Malkin was the best cop anyone could have been.

His performance was that of a "natural" cop—one of
perhaps 5 per cent of all police. These men and women come
to the job with an ability to make sound judgments about
particular people and situations, and they are also intuitively
able to choose the appropriate tools of police procedure.
Malkin had guns and a bullhorn at his disposal, and a hill
between him and his suspects. He chose to forego the force
and use the hill to make himself an equal rather than an
enemy of the people on top. By ascending the steep path in
full view and arriving breathless at the crest, the sergeant had

effectively disarmed the situation; the sweat on his forehead made him not so much a cop as everyman.

Sergeant Malkin was indeed everyman to citizens and to the patrolmen under his command. And most of the time his actions were those of a natural cop. Then about six months after the target practice episode Malkin was promoted to captain. The former captain had become chief when Kreins left for another department, and Malkin became that new chief's assistant. In short order he also became—the other officers complained—a disagreeable, arbitrary supervisor who nitpicked and rode his men unmercifully.

This new attitude was a complete turnabout from his behavior as sergeant, when he had taken a personal interest in the men and their morale, and had been willing to trust his own judgment as a leader. Captain Malkin, however, didn't make many decisions of his own. When Malkin's promotion was announced, former Chief Kreins congratulated him and advised him that "the captain's position requires complete loyalty to the chief." Malkin interpreted this to mean that he was not to exercise his judgment but simply to protect the chief's position and to carry out the chief's policies. Thus, Malkin submerged his own normal process of evaluation and withheld his natural interest in and communication with his subordinates. During that brief period, Dave Malkin was not his own man.

The word of Malkin's changed behavior reached me quickly. He was the object of snide remarks at a bull session, and later that morning one officer sought me out to report that "since being promoted, Dave Malkin has become an S.O.B." A few minutes later I passed Malkin in the hall and said I'd been hearing some unfavorable comments about him. He responded that he was aware of them, too, and he'd been meaning to talk with me about his new position.

We met the next day. "Doc, I feel like I'm on a treadmill. There's so much work to do as a captain that I can hardly keep up with it, and now I'm the one who has to pass along all the chief's new policies and rules. I know it's making me nervous and uptight, but I don't have time to be myself anymore."

I asked Malkin to explain his concept of the captain's role, and he said, "the chief's right arm." He also examined his attitude toward the new chief's methods of working and acknowledged that his impulse to give complete loyalty to the chief had led to this predicament. My advice to him was that his new job may require that he be an S.O.B., but he must be *his own* S.O.B.

We had several more meetings, generally discussing the same questions, during which Malkin developed a philosophical perspective of his situation. He was able to be more detached when administering the chief's decisions and to rely more on his own judgment in many instances. Soon he became less isolated from his subordinates, resuming the sports and social activities he'd enjoyed with them as a sergeant. His temporary crisis in being an effective leader was resolved through his willingness to examine and change his behavior.

I feel that this is one clear example of a psychiatrist's value to both the individual cop and the Sausalito department. Malkin is now chief of police in another small city, and I have kept in close touch with him as a friend and as a consultant for his department.

The performance of Sergeant Malkin and the need for counseling of Captain Malkin illustrate two of the three types of policemen I've seen in my twelve years in this work. In handling the target practice episode Malkin acted like a natural cop, combining judgment and police procedure in just the right proportions. When he faltered after being promoted, Malkin's performance was like that of the majority of police. Again, perhaps 60 per cent of cops fit this category: they are good at their work most of the time, but they need some continuing education and counseling to avoid succumbing to the intense pressures of their jobs. The third type of cop constitutes about 35 per cent of all police—he is the man who shouldn't even be in uniform. Often you need a psychiatrist to spot him.

The behavior of each of these types of policeman also can be illustrated by the choices Malkin faced in handling the incident on Wolfback Ridge. His leadership and decisions ranked him in the 5-per cent category of natural cops. If he had followed straight police procedure, surrounding the suspects and calling for them to surrender, he'd have been in the 60-per cent category (no matter how violent the confrontation). If he'd "shot first and asked questions later," as the cliché goes, or if he had become angry or afraid in the midst of the confrontation and put others on the defensive, he'd have been among the unacceptable 35 per cent of police.

Of course these distinctions are not always hard and fast—Malkin himself fit into two categories at different times. But generally a cop's personality and performance will place him in one slot, and this can almost always be determined through psychiatric screening. Unfortunately, it has not been possible for me to weed out the unsuitable cops who were never screened or to keep chiefs from employing people I've recommended against hiring. This is one primary reason for a psychiatric in-service program—to lessen the negative impact of people who shouldn't be cops on both the citizens and the department.

8
Surviving a Media Blitz

WE DIDN'T KNOW it at the time, but for two years our program was operating in a vacuum. At least that's how it seemed in contrast to what came next—a media blitz that gave the Sausalito police a combination of celebrity and notoriety, plus a lot more trouble than we had ever anticipated.

The men had long since become used to me and to the various aspects of the in-service psychiatric program, and new officers who joined the force readily accepted this as standard procedure. And though not common knowledge among citizens, my sessions were well known along the police grapevine, an informal communication network that helped create and fill openings in the Sausalito department. In fact, police from other communities were quick to apply whenever a position was vacant, and there was always an ample file of applications from people wanting to begin their police careers in Sausalito. Similarly, because our department enjoyed a good reputation among cities in the area— and the officers had the extra measure of training provided by the program—many of them moved on to higher-ranking, better-paying jobs elsewhere. So we had a regular turnover, but if anything, it was a credit to the department.

The storm of publicity that hit in late 1968 was intended to be a credit to the Sausalito police. But it didn't turn out that way. Instead of working in a vacuum, where we'd had problems, but our own problems, the men began to feel as if they were living in a fish bowl. It started with a brief mention of our program in a *Time* magazine essay on "Law and Order," and the word spread so quickly that the chief and I were deluged with requests for interviews and visits to the group sessions. National television and radio networks ran special reports on the program, and even the BBC and international editions of U. S. newspapers covered the Sausalito experiment.

Initially the fame was fun. All three television networks filmed a complete bull session (also attended by several reporters), and the men were spit and polished but otherwise pretty much themselves. Except for a few attempted jokes early in the meeting, we had a typically open, frank discussion. I was pleased that these cops were confident enough about themselves and the "rightness" of our sessions to reveal personal opinions and prejudices before the cameras.

The Summer Olympics had been held just prior to our meeting, and we started talking about the black athletes' having raised their fists in a salute after receiving their medals. The men's opinions were candid and varied: most officers felt the salute was disrespectful to the American flag—and American people—but some expressed sympathy with the athletes' desire to signify a racial identity as well as a national one. It was a good topic to get the men thinking, and as with many subjects we've discussed, the cops' feelings about this specific event led them to examine their general attitudes. By the end of the session several men had offered parallels between the athletes and something they'd encountered in their work.

Surviving a Media Blitz / 121

Unfortunately, the best parts of that meeting didn't make the news. The provocative, the sensational, the inflammatory, and the intimate details make news, and much of the coverage of this bull session emphasized these points. Instead of reporting that these cops' candid opinions served as a tool with which they could learn about themselves, the media accounts zoomed in on the opinions and summed it all up as "group therapy"! These stories praised the program and faithfully reported the increased arrest rate and the lack of complaints against officers in Sausalito, but they also tended to reinforce many readers' stereotypes about police. The television cameras were able to catch the spirit and intent of the program. But some newspaper reports, though well-intentioned, missed the point: they showed cops who had various degrees of prejudice without explaining that because the men were aware of their feelings, they would be much less likely to let those attitudes interfere with fair treatment of citizens in their work.

The next "event" we discussed at a bull session was the program's publicity. Though the men had enjoyed their moment in the spotlight, the people of Sausalito wouldn't let them forget their celebrity status. Suddenly these were elite cops from whom citizens expected special treatment or superhuman efforts. Some residents equated publicity about the in-service program with virtual elimination of crime and nuisances. When the burglaries didn't stop and the street people still filled the sidewalks and parks, certain residents dismissed the program as useless, or at least overpraised. Other people tried to test the "new" cops by calling them names or teasing them about the department's shrink. The question the police themselves had faced and resolved—"why do we need a psychiatrist?"—was now being thrown at them from all sides. The spate of publicity was an additional source of pressure for several months.

Most Sausalito cops recognized the value of the in-service

psychiatric program, but the publicity made a few men withdraw even more. Two men, in fact, remained hostile to me as long as they were in the department; a third warmed up a bit as the months passed and he wasn't singled out as crazy or anything equally embarrassing. But resistance to my work took various forms. One patrolman began leaving notes in my mailbox at home; at first these were slurs on me and my profession. Later he took to copying portions of stories from novels or magazines and demanding that I predict how the story would end. Although I knew who this man was—I could have guessed even if I hadn't recognized his handwriting—I was not able to confront him with this knowledge. In group sessions he was silent but not openly hostile, and his behavior on duty was not bad enough for the chief to insist that he see me for private counseling. To overcome his anger at me (or at what I represented to him) would have required his willing participation in individual sessions with me, and that was not likely to happen. He ignored the several openings I gave him to talk with me informally, and he'd have denied leaving the notes or harboring any resentment of me had I confronted him directly. This man transferred to another police agency about a year after my program began, and he left police work not long thereafter.

I couldn't get close enough to talk to that officer, but on other occasions my private sessions brought challenges from some cops. One man made several individual appointments with me, each time rather aggressively confronting me with details of his accomplishments as a policeman and stories of how people liked and praised him. When I inquired at each meeting why he felt it necessary to tell me all this, he replied that he didn't want to boast in front of the other officers and yet he thought he didn't get enough attention during our departmental sessions. In fact, he was reacting to his own insecurity, seeking approval from me in private that he feared he would not get in a group situation. In the course of

Surviving a Media Blitz / 123

several more meetings we did make progress, though; he learned to put less value on exploits or others' opinions and to accept his own rather modest stature in the department. This man was not a leader or an outstanding officer, but he was dependable and generally liked by the other police. Eventually he came to believe that.

Still another officer disagreed with my opinions about him and ultimately took me to court. By then I had begun consulting with several other police departments, and this man was a cop I hadn't screened in one of these new agencies. He was a rookie cop in a small department; his chief had referred him to me for counseling near the end of his probationary year. His performance as a policeman had been uneven at best; he suffered fits of depression during which he treated suspects roughly and refused to take orders from superiors. He also took a disproportionate amount of sick leave. He was not eager to discuss his failings as a cop, but he participated willingly in the standard psychotherapeutic interview. At a second meeting—required by the chief—he talked more about his family and childhood, but resisted any examination of his current problems on the force.

After our second meeting I wrote an evaluation of his personality, based on my psychotherapeutic interviews of him rather than on any discussion of his performance as a police officer. I sent the chief a short summary of my findings, pointing out that had this been a screening situation I'd have recommended against hiring this officer. A few days later the chief informed the man that he would not be kept on the force, and the officer promptly appealed this action. A police review committee agreed with the chief, so the officer filed suit against the city. Since the chief had consulted me before making his decision, I was asked to appear at the court hearing, where a judge would uphold or overrule the chief's action.

The officer's lawyer had some of the same objections to my

work with police that I'd heard from unsuccessful applicants and biased citizens or bureaucrats. First he questioned my qualifications: since I am both a neurologist and a psychiatrist, the attorney argued, how could I be adequately informed in two specialties? Then he tried to shoot down my interview technique as a basis for judging personality: how could I know enough about a man in one or two hours of talk to get him hired or fired? Why hadn't I used modern testing methods such as Rorschach or MMPI?

In answer to these queries I stated that my years of medical and psychiatric education had prepared me to make such analyses of personality; that my psychotherapeutic interview measured both personality and willingness to participate in self-examination; and that the psychometric test would only be of help if I could not arrive at a clear picture of someone's personality through use of the interview technique. The judge asked if I had any such difficulty evaluating the officer in question, and I replied that the man's psychological and emotional profile emerged distinctly during our two sessions, and that I stood by my previous recommendation to the chief. The suit was dismissed.

My private counseling of certain police also was influential in the development of rather strained relations with some police departments. As a result of all the publicity the Sausalito program received, I was asked to consult and screen police applicants for several other communities. Because I came to the new departments as a sort of phenomenon—my reputation for success in Sausalito had preceded me—a number of high-ranking officers felt confident about discussing their personal problems in private sessions. Perhaps they thought I could give them simple formulas for overcoming their hassles. Some of these police were disillusioned to learn that solving such problems required realistic awareness and constant attention. For a few men this disillusionment and embarrassment at my knowledge of their personal lives interfered with our working relationships. One chief simply stopped calling me to screen applicants; another was more candid when he said that he thought I was "too familiar with the personalities" in his department, and he feared that this might affect my opinions about new candidates. Though I assured this chief of my objectivity, I knew that my usefulness to both of these departments had been compromised. A chief often has difficulty following my recommendation not to hire someone who looks promising on paper or to a police committee; if that chief is uptight about his dealings with me, he's far less likely to give credence to my professional opinion.

In those instances my program did not have a chance to take hold because of a leader's reluctance. My relationships with other departments have ebbed and flowed, as the top positions and styles of leadership have changed. In several instances, though, I've begun to work with new departments because one of the men in my original Sausalito program has become a top officer there. Since 1968, I've screened approximately 1700 applicants for police work and given lectures to several thousand more law enforcement personnel. I've consulted extensively with eight departments—six in California, one in Michigan, one in Massachusetts—and maintain informal contact with a dozen others, and have responded to inquiries from such diverse nations as Turkey, Russia, Greece, West Germany, and Italy. In all of these places the issues and problems are the same—morale, corruption, budget cutbacks, cops' lack of knowledge about themselves and about others' behavior. My work has made a dent, but the limited amount I've been able to do only underscores the need for a psychiatric component in every police department, everywhere.

Part II

The preceding chapters trace the beginnings of my work with police and report the development of a psychiatric in-service training program. During the twelve years I've worked closely with law enforcement personnel, I've learned what type of person goes into this work and who succeeds as a cop; how police departments function as parts of city governments and as self-contained units; the difference between crime as defined by law and as enforced by police; and the useful elements in police tradition and organization that could help to make every cop a professional. The following chapters explore these concerns, which are likely to affect each of us in the future. The policeman is the only member of our increasingly complex society who can use his weapons, force, and authority at his personal discretion; thus, we must look at him—his job, his personality, his mental state—with closer scrutiny than we ever have before.

9
Cops and Their Families

A COP IS USUALLY a certain type of person. The motivation for helping people—the rescue fantasy—is always there, whether the police officer's personality could be considered *sublimated* (rescue fantasy faced and resolved) or *reactive* (rescue fantasy unresolved, perhaps unrecognized). But the majority of police also share other common characteristics that have been revealed in my interviews and in surveys of various law enforcement groups. For example, a cop—man or woman—generally is gregarious, a team player who places high value on loyalty to the organization he or she represents. Police usually come from a strong religious background, often Catholic, and most cops believe in society's traditional values of respect for parents, marriage and rearing of children, adherence to moral codes, and love of country.

The person who chooses police work is likely to prefer working with his hands and with other people to introspective or intellectual endeavors. The cop also likes a definite structure to his job, a pattern that organizes the external forces of his working life and gives him a sense of security. This is not to say that learning such a job is easy or that police work is repetitious and predictable—it is anything but monotonous or uncomplicated. But this sort of work offers just the right setting for the person who is oriented toward helping others as part of a team: the work shifts may change from month to month, but a cop knows what he will be doing and with whom; he has the symbol of his work in his uniform, in which all but the most troubled cops take some pride; he knows that his community's laws are behind his authority and actions; and at times he feels the camaraderie of knowing that even if the public and the politicians are criticizing the police, he and his colleagues are together against the world.

A survey taken a few years ago in the San Francisco department offers a similar and more specific profile of the average cop. He is a man, thirty-six years old, married with three children. His wife works (her salary was not reported); he makes $1,106 per month. He has spent two years in military service and has taken college courses but does not have a degree. He joined the police department at age twenty-one. He goes to church regularly and belongs to one or more fraternal organizations. His wife and other relatives worry about his being in police work; the chances are nine out of ten that his wife has asked him to change careers. He doesn't change jobs. It takes him thirteen years to make sergeant, several more years to make lieutenant, on the average. He doesn't think he has an equal opportunity for future advancement within the department, though, because of political favoritism at the higher levels.

Since that survey was taken, the average salary has gone up several hundred dollars per month and the educational level of police has improved; otherwise it's quite accurate.

The circumstances that produce a person's motivation to become a cop, that is, the predominance of the rescue fantasy at a crucial period in his development as a child, also govern the sort of police officer this person becomes. For example, although police generally are team players, some of them feel the need to win admiration or prove their loyalty by feats of heroism. Usually this is just what the other cops don't need. If a man repeatedly takes chances by driving dangerously to catch a suspect's car (which could have been intercepted ahead by another police unit) or by trying to subdue armed suspects without assistance when he could have waited for help, he is acting out complex inner urges derived from his psychological development. Whatever his unconscious reasons, a cop who wants to play hero is feared by most of his colleagues, because his injudicious actions could very easily get them or innocent citizens hurt or killed.

Certain circumstances of their lives cause some police to act in definite ways, and if those circumstances change, their behavior can change just as abruptly. I saw many instances of this in the departments where I've consulted; some men's performance and attitudes improved after major changes in their lives, and some cops just deteriorated. One young man whom I'd screened was a borderline case—I had suggested that if he were hired he would need a firm hand in training and supervision. He was hired and received good training during his probationary year. His performance had been undistinguished but certainly acceptable as one of the 60 per cent of police who are basically all right. My cautious recommendation about him had been based on his somewhat confused reasoning as to why he wanted to be a police officer. His background did include the basis for rescue-fantasy motivation, but he was also reacting against a specific family situation. His father was involved in organized crime in the Midwest, and this young man had long been disgusted and frightened by his father's activities and associates. Yet even though his interest in law enforcement was partly reactionary, he was not overzealous or punitive as a cop himself.

Just before he was to be hired permanently, however, his

father was murdered in a gangland-style shooting. The cop's life changed instantly; the object of his fear and reaction—his father—had been removed, and the feelings that had been guiding him as a cop gave way to confusion. He didn't show up for work for several days, refused help from friends, and when he finally returned to the job he was almost useless. He came to see me at the chief's suggestion but was uncommunicative. Consequently, he was not made a permanent member of the department and is no longer in police work.

This cop's story is a good example of the imprecision with which a police psychiatrist must work at times. The man was a borderline case, but I felt he was worth hiring and training and the chief shared my view. He was given the guidance I recommended and performed well in his job for a year. Then an important influence on him changed abruptly, and his delicate balance of motivation and training fell apart. That department lost a good man, through circumstances that none of us could control or predict.

An officer in another department was an example of just the opposite situation This man had been hired before any screening was in effect, and he was far from the ideal cop. He had some responsibilities for training recruits, and he bullied the new officers, never missing a chance to embarrass them in front of their peers. This man's attitude toward his fellow police was little better, and he was especially hostile to women. His problems were complicated by a serious drinking problem, which affected his performance as a cop even though he was not known to be drunk on the job.

The chief suggested to this officer that I might have some suggestions for him to improve his supervisory duties, since he would not have been willing to meet with me to discuss his personal problems. We met several times, and at the final session I told him that his behavior was not consistent with good police work or with setting a decent example for recruits. He responded with anger, daring me to try to get his badge.

A few months later his father died (of natural causes), and the change in his attitudes and behavior was swift and surprising. He stopped drinking, took an immediate interest in improving his work, and began dating a woman whom he married later that year. Although I have not discussed this officer's feelings with him, it seems clear to me that his hostility and uncertainty were somehow associated with his father. When that family situation changed, his behavior made an about-face. In this instance the department and the community benefited from a change in circumstances beyond their control. This man is a rare example of a bad cop who became a good one.

Of course the circumstances of a cop's work can bring about changes in his attitudes and behavior. Most often, though, such changes are gradual, such as drinking to relax, which becomes a drinking problem and later may become an addiction to alcohol. In fact, alcoholism among police is one of the most common and most devastating problems facing communities today. And the tendency toward heavy use of this drug results in large measure from the pressures of police work.

Although a cop is where he wants to be—in a job that permits him to help others, as part of a team effort—there is constant tension in his work. Almost all of the people with whom he must deal are troubled, because they have been victims of some crime, or have been accused of committing a crime, or are simply out of step with society's march. Whatever the situation, the cop usually bears the brunt of the person's hostility, despite the fact that he is there to offer assistance. The citizen whose car has been stolen or whose store has been held up demands to know why the police weren't patroling at that very moment; the same person being given a ticket for speeding wishes the cops would get off the streets altogether.

The policeman who answers a call that a violent family argument is taking place may be assaulted—literally or figuratively—from all sides. The husband doesn't want a cop telling him to quiet down and stop threatening his wife or children; the wife fears that any intervention will just make the situation worse. If one family member has a gun or other weapon, the officer may be injured while trying to confiscate it, or even his presence may cause someone to use that weapon. In fact, family disturbances account for one-third of all police deaths.

So the cop must include crisis intervention among his routine duties. He will have to endure the pressure of knowing he often must go into explosive situations where he'll be greeted with hostility. Usually he can defuse such situations with a minimum of injury to anyone, but he seldom gets any thanks for his efforts.

Yet his concern almost always pays off for the people involved, and sometimes they do let the officer know it. A man who had transferred from a county sheriff's department to the Sausalito police told me about such an instance. He was riding alone on patrol and saw a brand-new car pulled off on the shoulder of the highway, miles from any gas station or other assistance. "I thought these people might need help," he told me, "so I pulled up behind them and walked toward the car. A man was behind the wheel and a woman was in the passenger seat. Before I could reach their car, the woman jumped out and ran up to me, saying, 'Take me away, Officer.' She and her husband had been arguing, talking about splitting up. I was able to get them to come with me to the station and talk about things calmly, where they weren't in such cramped quarters and he couldn't get in a wreck if he decided to take off in the car while he was still so angry. After an hour I drove them back to their car, and they were much more relaxed. Two days later I got a very nice letter from the man, thanking me for stopping and making them talk through their anger before they took it out on the highway or something. There was a P. S. that said, 'You missed your calling. You should have been a marriage counselor instead of a deputy sheriff.' "

Such expressions of thanks are few in a cop's daily life, and between them comes a galaxy of complaints. In addition, every policeman has certain personal fears that go with his job. These concerns make some cops jumpy or irritable; they affect others less visibly, but contribute to the potential for any officer to lose his self-control at a critical moment.

The most obvious concern is the danger associated with any form of law enforcement. Actually, a cop spends a relatively small proportion of his work time at risk of being killed or injured—perhaps 15 per cent—but every officer goes into this job knowing that the risks are there. The undercurrent of tension that accompanies this knowledge is compounded by the randomness of violence that happens to police officers. Only the rarest of cops are sought out by gangsters who want revenge, for example; the vast majority of police deaths or injuries are not personal and very often are not intentional.

A closely related fear among police is that their own safety might be jeopardized by another cop. As I have noted, nobody wants a hero for a partner, because of that person's tendency to take risks in defiance of accepted procedure or even common sense. And police worry, too, about a partner or backup officer who might freeze at the moment of greatest danger, the person who couldn't bring himself to fire at a suspect or to enter an area where gunfire is being exchanged. At such times training and discipline must take precedence over personal emotions, yet many cops' behavior on the job is not steady enough to assure their colleagues that they can be depended upon in a tight spot.

In fact, many officers have asked my opinion of other cops—whether a certain man could be relied upon to back up his fellow police. In many cases I really don't know, but regardless of my own information, I always decline to predict anyone's behavior to his colleagues. This would only undermine the morale among officers, and my own means of helping prevent disasters of unreliability is to educate all the men to their weaknesses and particular stresses. The best way to instill confidence in a person—including a cop—is to guide him toward self-knowledge, so that he can understand his fears or anger and intercept any emotional reaction that might threaten his performance.

The public's attitude toward police in general is another source of frustration for cops. Because they deal most often with troubled people who seldom relate to cops in rational, human ways, police tend to be isolated from the rest of the community. So they stick together, which is not always beneficial. The same officer who might express his concern to me that another cop could not be depended upon in a dangerous situation probably would defend that man's actions to anyone outside the department. This is one reason why alcoholics or pathological cops aren't drummed out of the force, or at least removed from street duties. The police see themselves as beleaguered, and when charges of brutality or irresponsibility are leveled at one of their own, they generally close ranks to protect that member instead of examining his behavior and taking corrective action.

An important contributing factor to the cop's sense of isolation is the seeming ineffectiveness of the judicial system. Recently one sergeant observed that "Justice ends with the arrest. The dope pusher, the burglar, even the murderer can find a smart lawyer and get off on a technicality. And even if they don't have a lawyer, the judge can send them back on the street for months or years before their trials come up."

Police feel similarly hamstrung by the complex rules of evidence and arrest procedures they must follow if an arrest is to result in prosecution and punishment for someone found guilty. Although cops realize the necessity of such safeguards for innocent persons who have been wrongly accused, they are often disappointed when their efforts are thwarted by those very rules. Unfortunately, some police may react immaturely to this frustration by circumventing the safeguards. There are even instances of officers shooting a suspect whom they believe to be guilty.

The sense of isolation that touches many police may also influence them to accept favors from certain segments of the community. Because of their work and their authority, cops are routinely subjected to temptations that I call the three B's—booze, broads, and bribes. That is, the pressure of the job may lead to their drinking while on duty (perhaps accepting free drinks at bars or restaurants on their beats); many police, in the line of duty, have daily contact with persons who wish to become sexually involved with them; and any number of persons would be willing to bribe a cop to have him ignore some offense or criminal activity. For many these temptations become harder to resist as time goes by: middle-aged officers seem especially vulnerable in this regard.

Some other concerns of police stem from their family backgrounds. The same circumstances that resulted in a cop's motivation to help others also have made some men sensitive about their masculinity. The officer who grew up in a household where his father was very abusive or very weak might sense the need to rescue one parent and consequently confuse his own masculine identity. Such a man may fear that he is homosexual, even if he is married and has healthy relationships with women. This fear makes some police uptight at the mention of the subject and perhaps even brutal to homosexuals with whom they must deal on the job. Of course this situation applies to only a small number of police, and very few have discussed it with me. But their sensitivity can be observed and the reasons for it explained through examination of their backgrounds.

Although the fear of being homosexual does not affect all

police, every cop does worry about his family. And the dangers of his job are magnified when he wonders how his family would get along if he were killed or badly injured. The many sources of temptation for him may also lead to his feeling guilty about his family—if he takes sexual favors or begins to drink heavily, that guilt may erode his family life. Even if a cop doesn't give in to the temptations that come with the job (and most don't), he may have serious problems in relationships with his wife and children because of the constant pressures he feels about his work.

A subtle factor in this web of interrelated fears is the type of person a police officer chooses to marry. Whether the cop is a man or woman, the rescue-fantasy motivation will strongly influence his or her choice of a mate. Usually the same need to "rescue" a parent that the officer felt as a child will be transferred to his partner. One obvious example is the cop who arrested a prostitute, became interested in helping her, and ended up marrying her. That was an effective rescue, and an example of two personalities who needed each other—though I don't know how the marriage has fared.

Such a strong need to help his mate does not always make a good marriage. The combination of the policeman's work and the interdependence of personalities leads to marital problems for many police. One significant problem I've discussed with police wives—after their initial embarrassment about revealing family problems—is their husbands' sexual performance. For some wives the problem has been that the man does not want sex or is impotent, which usually is the result of tensions associated with his job. Other wives cannot ignore their own worries about whether their husbands are having sex with prostitutes or other women, and this suspicion affects their attitude toward marital relations. Resolution or even discussion of these problems is often difficult for a cop and his wife (or a cop and her husband), precisely because of the types of people they are. That is, the need to help others that motivates a police officer affects his or her choice of spouse and relationship to the spouse. Confronting marital problems may confuse the cop's perspective and make him or her less secure, thus damaging the relationship further.

Of course a cop's family is subjected to the same isolation he feels—from friends who make wisecracks about "pigs" to wives and children being excluded from social groups. The stigma associated with police work is one reason why most wives ask their husbands to change careers. One young officer told me that his wife had refused to have sex with him until he quit the force. She hated the way she and her children were treated by others in their community, and she couldn't shut off her fears about whether her husband would come home from his next shift. In some instances I've been able to work on these problems with couples and with groups of wives. Although this cannot solve their marital difficulties immediately, frequent discussion and attention will help alleviate the tensions at home and may lead to mature acceptance of the realities of a cop's life by both husband and wife.

Still another area of concern for most police is their children. Particularly during the last decade, cops have seen thousands of young people strung out on drugs, sleeping in parks and on streets, totally alienated from their families and from traditional societal values. They fear that their own children will "drop out," and they don't know how to steer the youngsters away from these influences. The fact that these are children of police makes the situation more touchy, because a son or daughter may choose to rebel against his or her parents by resisting the authority the police-parent stands for—in short, by breaking the law in some major way.

Finally, a cop's family worries are augmented by his changing work schedule. If he is a patrolman, he will change shifts several times during the year, probably just as the family routine was adjusting to his hours. If he is a supervisor or detective, he may have to work overtime a great deal, causing resentment or frustration on the part of a wife and children who seldom see him. Of course these problems are not unique to police, but taken together with his other pressures, they serve to complicate a job the cop feels he must do.

It's a sort of vicious circle, a set of fears that won't go away and a type of person who won't change his line of work. But if that person is stable, has a mature perspective that includes discussing his problems with his family, and takes genuine pride in his integrity as a law officer, he can cope with the concerns and remain a healthy, effective individual—who just happens to be a cop.

10
Cops and Their Department

A WELL-ORGANIZED department is essential to effective law enforcement, but at times that very organization can be detrimental to the public and to individual police officers.

The military structure that police departments have always employed has both strengths and weaknesses. Its principal advantages are that lines of authority are clear, and training and discipline must be maintained by all members. Police work involves many situations in which the military form of instant response to orders or training can save lives and prevent chaos. For example, the San Francisco Police reacted automatically and properly to instructions when a would-be assassin fired a pistol at President Ford in September 1975. The cops had been lining the curb along the street where the President's motorcade was about to depart, keeping spectators from overflowing the crowded sidewalks. When a shot rang out, the police instantly joined hands or held extended nightsticks to contain the surging, frightened crowd. The cops' quick action made it possible for the President's limousine and escort to speed away from the scene and provided access for any emergency vehicles had they been needed. Police who were close to the assailant subdued her (with assistance from citizens), but the officers who were not nearby stood their ground, rather than plunging into the crowd or leaving their posts for a better view elsewhere. The handling of this incident was a model of appropriate, disciplined police service.

Yet the military structure of law enforcement agencies also leaves much room for corruption. In some large urban departments it is staggering: a 1972 study revealed that one out of three police in Chicago was guilty of a criminal act; one out of four in Boston; and one of five in Washington, D.C. These crimes included assault, theft, shakedown and extortion, and acceptance of bribes. Despite efforts to purge police criminals, these proportions probably have not changed appreciably in the last five years.

It is probably no coincidence that the number of police criminals in some departments mirrors the number of bad cops—the 35 per cent who are psychologically unfit for police work. Certainly the index of corruption among police cannot be reduced significantly until the bad cops are removed from their positions. As it is now, these bad cops simply continue the problem by abusing the rights of citizens and prolonging the unfavorable public attitudes toward police. Worse, because the very structure of most departments encourages advancement on the basis of seniority, the longer bad cops are permitted to stay, the more influence they will have on recruits who depend on older officers to teach them the ropes during the first crucial year.

Thus, although police corruption is the product of a variety of factors, I believe there are many problems in the military organization of police that make departments inherently corruptible. This is not to say that the military chain of command should be abandoned; rather, it is the areas of vulnerability in that chain that need constant vigilance.

Because authority moves from the top down, officers at all subordinate levels of leadership—chiefs, captains, lieutenants, and sergeants—must be trustworthy and efficient. Yet a key position in this structure, the position of sergeant, is often the weakest link in the chain. In most departments a sergeant is in charge of each of three shifts, and police recruits are generally divided among them so that experienced officers will always be working each shift as well. The sergeant is supposed to supervise all officers on the shift and to evaluate the performance of the rookies under him. Thus, he must know the patrolman's duties and be able to determine how well a recruit is performing, and he must have the judgment and interest to help a rookie improve his work when necessary. He should be extremely watchful for signs of corruption on the beat—the "broads, booze, and bribes" temptations I discussed in Chapter 9—and handle them firmly and immediately.

All too often, though, poor patrolmen have been promoted to the rank of sergeant, perhaps only to get them off the street (and thus minimize complaints about their work). The man who was an ineffective street cop is expected to tell other police how to do their jobs. In many instances I've seen rookies whom I had considered borderline candidates placed under a tough, authoritarian sergeant—just the opposite of the sort of supervisor I had recommended. One young man had good potential as a policeman, although he needed firm guidance from a mature leader. But he was assigned to a militaristic, overly aggressive sergeant who encouraged him to draw his gun or use his nightstick to display his authority. It was no surprise that in his two years on the force, the rookie accidentally shot himself twice and wounded a civilian. This young man, a potentially good cop, was developed into a bad one, and the only real improvement in his situation will be if he leaves police work.

Another corruptive influence at the sergeant level in many

police departments stems from the particular types of policemen who were hired in the mid-1960s, when campus riots and public demonstrations brought about a backlash of authoritarian sentiment. I have recently seen many of these officers in my classes for sergeants, and they represent a distinct difference from the men who made up the sergeant groups prior to the mid-1970s. The new breed of sergeant is more likely to be among the 35 per cent of police I call "untreatable" cops—inflexible, repressive, psychologically unstable. Consequently, we can expect a correspondingly higher rate of rookie cops being poorly trained—or even lost to effective service through corrupting influences—because of the increasing ratio of unsuitable men supervising them as sergeants. Fortunately, this trend appears to be temporary, since police hiring and training standards have become more stringent and psychological screening is in use. But many departments and communities will feel the effects of this impulse for authority for years to come.

The manner in which promotions are made is also vulnerable to departmental corruption. Too often favoritism, seniority, cliquishness, or subtle forms of bribery form the basis of promotion and lead to internal power struggles and trade-offs. The criteria for promotion must include competence as a police officer and as a supervisor, ability to train subordinates, and psychological stability. Like the bad sergeant, the troubled or corrupt officer who holds a leadership position in a department has the potential to harm or misguide many recruits or subordinates—and the damage he might do increases with the importance of his position.

One way to combat these improper promotion methods is to establish a rigorous screening of officers *before* promotions are made, somewhat similar to the way the Sausalito department hired Chief Kreins in 1966. This process includes psychological screening and interviews by committees of police and citizens. The interviews provide an important forum where concerned, experienced persons, whose skills are related to the police officer's job, can question the candidate on specific details about police work. They provide an excellent complement to psychiatric screening—and they should be established at all levels of hiring from recruit to chief. In fact, the "oral boards," as these committees are called, often catch subtleties of personality that written exams and even the psychotherapeutic interview might miss.

Optimally the oral interview committees should always include at least one private citizen; in one instance that I recall such a person recognized a problem that no one else had considered. The civilian member wanted to know if the applicant being interviewed had been married more than once. Through further questioning, he admitted that he had been married six times, all for less than two years. This prompted the citizen member to insist that the chief check further into the man's background, whereupon it was discovered that this otherwise promising applicant was a wife-beater.

At another oral interview a police officer noticed that the applicant had a nervous habit of rubbing his nose in a certain way. The cop watched the candidate until the interview was about to conclude, then interrupted to ask: "Are you a sniffer?" The applicant was surprised and embarrassed, and he reluctantly said "Yes." He revealed that he had used cocaine regularly for several months and had been questioned by another police department about his association with drug dealers. Yet these facts had not been uncovered in the preliminary background check about the applicant—they came to light because an alert cop saw a gesture he recognized.

Screening an applicant for promotion is just as valuable as screening a candidate for recruitment, but it is only one step. Another means of countering corruption before it takes hold is limiting a captain's or lieutenant's length of service in any one post. Today in most departments, one man may be precinct captain for twenty years, with the accompanying trade-off of favors and obligations that longevity in power usually brings. And the captains who have run their own district stations for many years are most often the ones who resist any change proposed or mandated by the chief or other departmental administrators. This resistance often augments the split between "downtown" administrators and the beat cops, who regularly hear their captains' or sergeants' complaints about the chief and his staff.

We could do well to examine the British police system, where there is little crime among the officers. One reason is that precinct captains are assigned to a station for no more than three years. Because the pecking order changes regularly, criminal elements that seek to influence police operations are frustrated. In the United States, this system could be adapted to most police departments. By shifting high-level officers from one assignment to another at fairly frequent intervals—once a year, for instance—a chief can keep a "buddy system" or corrupt administration from taking hold.

The cop who is *not* promoted—or doesn't wish to be—may also bring corruption into a department. Ideally, no man over forty years old should be walking a beat: he increasingly becomes a hazard to himself and others because his physical agility has declined and because his personal frustrations (fear of responsibility, family obligations, financial problems) rise rather spectacularly after that age. If he has not made a supervisory rank—sergeant or above—by age forty, he is questionably effective as a cop and is more prone to the temptations of corruption he faces daily on the street. Worse still, he may have a lucrative criminal sideline working for him on his beat.

Some of these patrolmen should be taken off all police duty—forced to retire or even terminated, if criminal activity can be documented. Others could be transferred to less volatile jobs, such as traffic positions, booking detail, guard service, file and evidence control.

Such policies as taking patrolmen off their beats or reassigning captains are the chief's domain. He is the department's source of authority and its instrument of reform. And the time for reform usually is ripe when there is to be a change of chiefs within a police department. If the chief who is leaving has been in power for a long time, chances are that some form of corruption has crept into the organization. If the departing chief has been in command for only a short time, he may have been forced out or simply have given up because corruption and favoritism were already too entrenched in the department. In either case, the new leader is going to have to clean house.

For these reasons, a new chief should not come from within the ranks of his department. Although small departments such as Sausalito's may promote from within and suffer no severe consequences, this procedure is not advisable unless the residents and city officials are confident that their police are free of corruption. Otherwise, this action would simply preserve and perhaps enlarge the network of cronyism and favored treatment that existed when the new chief was a captain or lieutenant in the same department.

For large urban police forces, selection of a new chief from among the ranks is virtually unacceptable. What a department needs at the crucial point of change in administration is a thorough examination by a dispassionate eye, someone who has the knowledge to spot entrenched power or corruption and the guts to root it out. Such a person must also recognize the good cops and good leaders on his force and place them in positions where they can influence the training of new police and the operation of the department itself.

Similarly, an outgoing chief should not recommend his successor. His tenure is up, and anyone he chooses might try to emulate him, which could be just the wrong style of leadership for the natural talents of the new chief. And even if the new leader didn't act out his gratitude by adopting his predecessor's methods and policies, the same patterns of power and possible corruption could continue unchecked. This is one important reason why the person who is appointed acting chief when a chief leaves a department should not be chosen as permanent leader. The search outside the department for a new chief, and the passing over of an acting chief for an outsider, often angers both the department's rank and file and local residents or politicians. It may be difficult for these groups to think of the selection of the new chief in terms of the best person available anywhere, because their special interests might not be served by a new leader.

To become chief of a respected department, a cop must be both strong and ambitious. His strength will keep him from succumbing to the pressures of critical politicians or meddling citizens, but his ambition may grow to become detrimental to the department. For example, one chief with whom I worked some time ago had political aspirations of his own—he wanted to be elected to a county-wide law enforcement position, and his primary interest in being chief of a small department was to build a political power base from which to launch his campaign. He demanded intense loyalty from his associates and cultivated local business and civic leaders as confidants and friends. His bid for election was unsuccessful, but he did succeed in undermining public respect and trust for his department during his tenure as chief.

The changing public mood and its impact on police services and hiring practices can be poison for a department and is in itself a pernicious form of corruption. Too often influential citizens can bring pressure on the chief to drop or reduce a criminal charge or to change his procedures in some way.

There was a classic episode of this sort in one of the departments I worked with several years ago: a prominent citizen was arrested for drunk driving and because he was abusive and resistant, the man was handcuffed and taken to the police station. The two officers who made the arrest followed standard procedures and used only the force necessary to subdue their prisoner at the time of his arrest. But this citizen screamed bloody murder, charging that he had been handled brutally and arrested unfairly. Because he was well known in the community and in neighboring San Francisco, his charges were given plenty of media coverage—little of it favorable to the police department that had done its duty properly.

The officers were furious. It appeared that the chief and city officials were siding with the citizen who had made the charges, because their only public comments were that they would conduct a thorough investigation. The cops felt betrayed by their leaders and assaulted by the public, and they wanted some kind of forum to restore respect for their steady, efficient work. During a long, noisy bull session, the cops agreed that a meeting with the mayor, the city manager, and the chief was needed. After a few phone calls and juggled schedules, the chief arranged that meeting. This session was set to coincide with my regular formal lecture, where the men knew that they could voice their concerns in no uncertain terms. The chief completed his questioning of the officers involved during this session, and the mayor and city manager were convinced that the arrest had been legitimate and had involved no brutality or even rough treatment of the big shot. That afternoon the mayor and city manager released statements that their police had been in the right, and the chief confirmed this finding. The newspapers finally reported the cops' side of the story, with full support from city officials, and the men accepted their belated vindication. A few weeks later the indignant citizen quietly pleaded no contest to the charge and was given a stiff fine.

In this instance the chief investigated and backed up his officers against public criticism. In fact, the chief of any department must often be a buffer between politicians and the police, which is another good reason for his selection from outside the department. That way he will be totally objective about where the skeletons are buried, be they the cops' own secrets or those of political hacks who might wish to influence him.

Politicians' efforts at influencing the police chief or his officers may also backfire in very nasty ways. Many police are privy to confidential information about the city's leaders, whether it is official police records or mere rumor. So the cops and the politicians often have a standoff—if a councilman tries to cut the police budget or makes accusations of corruption within the department, he may find his personal dirty laundry being aired in public.

This kind of blackmail among public officials and law enforcement personnel is unhealthy for any community. If used, it may at least spark some reform within the department along with the ensuing scandal: if unused, the rumors and charges just fester until one side gives way. In either case, such political "little black books," like rumor and gossip, are hard to eliminate from the organization.

Attempts at intimidation of police by prominent citizens and politicians and cops trying to blackmail each other are characteristic of all levels of law enforcement. It should be no news to anyone that when Clarence Kelly took over administration of the FBI, his efforts at reform were frustrated by pockets of entrenched power and continuing revelations of unlawful activities by agents and by the original leaders of the bureau.

Cops do make an effort at policing themselves, however. Most large departments have an internal affairs bureau whose members investigate charges of wrongdoing by police or situations in which cops did not use accepted police procedures. If an officer shoots and kills a fleeing robbery suspect, for example, the internal affairs inspectors will try to determine the circumstances of the incident: was the suspect armed, or did the officer have reason to believe that his own safety or that of others was threatened? Customarily the officer whose conduct is being investigated is suspended from duty and his gun is kept at headquarters until the matter is resolved. He may be disciplined, transferred, or even fired if his actions are found to be negligent or intentionally violent, or the investigation may determine that the cop acted responsibly in the situation. (Public doubts may be difficult to assuage, though—citizens often want to believe the worst about police motives and actions. This is another strong justification for a department to maintain an independent internal affairs unit.)

Yet many police resent the power and secrecy associated with the internal affairs unit. They believe that the unit's officers often play favorites, excusing some cops and punishing others unfairly—often on the basis of personality rather than performance. Consequently, the chief must keep in close contact with the internal affairs unit and ensure that departmental policies are being administered equitably and thoroughly.

Self-policing is essential to a good department, but perhaps the most obvious indicator of excellence is the overall performance of the police. Certain specific criteria can be applied to measure performance, and these good or bad points can be easily recognized by both specialists and plain citizens. For instance, a good police force will answer every call that comes in, and its average response time will be two to five minutes from receipt of the call to arrival on the scene. Many outside factors may influence specific situations, but an average of a day's or a week's police calls and response times will determine whether a department meets these criteria. At present, many small and medium-sized departments do respond to calls this quickly, but few if any large urban departments even come close to this objective. In fact, less important calls (as defined by the sergeant in charge at a precinct station or by patrolmen on the street) often are never answered in major cities. One excuse police officers give is that they need to be ready to answer more urgent calls, or they may plead lack of manpower or poor communications for their failure to follow up on citizen complaints.

Some cops take the attitude that it's useless to investigate a car theft or minor burglary, for instance, because the chances of recovering the stolen property are almost nil. Their involvement in such matters usually is limited to taking the required report so that the victim can file an insurance claim, and very often they will tell the citizen exactly this. Yet in Sausalito, where loss of articles from burglaries reached a staggering $500,000 in 1962 during the administration of an uninterested chief, we brought losses down to just $63,000 in 1970. And because the Sausalito police do investigate and follow up on all reports, the department recovers an average of 75 per cent of stolen goods, as opposed to an average recovery rate of 20 per cent for most cities.

Another major area of performance for a police department is regard for human rights. This is where many departments fall down, either because of a general attitude of disrespect for suspects or because of the hostile treatment of citizens by a few troubled officers. Neglect of human rights can occur at any stage of contact between police and citizens. For example, a resident may call police to complain his neighbors are having a loud party, complete with blasting rock and roll music. The police go to the area, discover that the noise is coming from a house occupied by a number of young persons, and enter the house angrily, perhaps breaking up furniture in a search for supposed drugs or arresting everyone there. This is an instance of cops' reacting to their own prejudices, rather than treating all citizens with equal respect. If the party had been noisy executives and their wives or girl friends, the visit by those particular cops might have been quite different.

The police who book and handle suspects at the local jail also can greatly abuse human rights, even if they do not go beyond the limits of law. Prisoners can legally be searched for weapons and contraband, and some jailers conduct these searches in the most demeaning ways possible. The suspects may be left to wait for hours without being allowed to contact their families or attorneys, and at times a malicious jailer will strip a prisoner for a search, then wait several hours to perform that search. Some county prisons are notorious for such practices, and often the rate of prisoner escape attempts and even suicides soars because of it.

Similarly, the cops' handling of juvenile offenders or suspects offers a good index to their real attitudes toward crime and toward the community. Most police care a lot about kids and try to keep them out of juvenile detention halls, where a young person is more likely to learn how to continue a life of crime than to be rehabilitated. But some police assume that a kid whose neighbor accuses him of stealing something is automatically guilty, and these cops give that message to the youngster. Such tactics may lead the juvenile to defy the law because he feels that the police already consider him a criminal. At the very least this young person loses confidence in law enforcement.

The abusive attitudes of some police may not be obvious to anyone who hasn't dealt with such an officer, but there are certain signs of the internal problems in a department that can affect any police officer's sense of himself, his job, and his department. Morale is often low among cops in a poorly run department, and the officers' appearance usually reflects

Cops and Their Departments / 153

this. If the cops' dress varies from man to man—some in summer uniforms, some in winter clothing—or if police don't wear their badges, these officers are not being well supervised and have no incentive to care about their appearance. Likewise, consistent but sloppy dress, such as uniforms that are not cleaned or pressed, also may indicate a lack of pride among the police.

Finally, the members of a good department do not need to use sneaky tactics to make arrests or to give out some minimum number of tickets to citizens. Yet many departments retain such practices as "jackrabbiting," a maneuver in which a cop waits behind a barrier for a driver to take a liberty with the traffic laws, such as not making a complete stop at a stop sign, then darts out after him and gives a citation. Another such tactic is known as "sandbagging," which is among the nastiest of police practices. An officer will wait around the corner from a local bar at closing time and watch for drunken patrons to emerge. Instead of intercepting the inebriated citizen and calling a cab or driving him home, the cop will wait until the customer gets into his car and drives off, then chase him down and arrest this person for drunk driving.

Such tactics quickly turn public sentiment against the police, and no amount of "community relations" will restore the citizens' respect. In fact, "community relations" is a rather hollow term, at least when applied to police. There should be an atmosphere of trust between law enforcement agencies and citizens, and a well-run department whose officers truly care about their work will not need public relations programs or gimmicks. Rather, the cops themselves can win public respect by treating all persons fairly and refraining from abusive or underhanded practices.

Police, too, have an excellent opportunity to inform citizens about their work. A conversation I once had with a rookie cop illustrates this point. This officer came to a bull session quite bothered because he had been chewed out by a resident for allowing an illegally parked car to block that person's driveway. The resident had not called police but waited until he saw a squad car passing and hailed it, immediately launching a tirade of criticism at the officer. I asked the young policeman how he'd handled this, and he said he had apologized to the resident and called a tow truck to remove the car. Both men had gone away angry, though. I asked what the cop would have liked to do in that situation, and he confessed that he'd like to have "hit the guy in the mouth."

"What would that get you?" I inquired.

"A brutality charge."

"How else might you have handled it?"

"Well, I guess I might have told him according to the law I can't legally ticket a car on the street until it's been there for seventy-two hours unless he calls to complain about it. I also could have told him what I thought when I saw the car there—that it belonged to him or to someone visiting his house. I guess the point you're trying to make is that the citizen isn't going to know this kind of stuff if we don't tell him."

11
Cops and Their Profession

BECAUSE ALL POLICE departments have felt the pinch of inflated costs and lower budgets, cops have formed their own lobbying groups in many communities. Most medium-sized or large departments have one or more police associations, which have gained power and influence among rank and file cops as their demands for salary increases and better working conditions have gone unmet. For all practical purposes these associations are labor unions, even if they are not connected with traditional labor organizations. In some communities, police actually have joined traditional unions, such as the AFL-CIO, and in a number of small towns, the Teamsters.

But police unions are a step backward. This trend among police has resulted from frustration, to be sure; cops resent being treated as civil servants, with little or no special pay or distinction for their skills and risks, and their efforts at gaining professional recognition from public officials or citizens have gone nowhere. In many instances, however, standard labor movement tactics such as threatened strikes or work slowdowns have simply increased public and official discontent with the police position, rather than gaining them any favor. A 1975 police strike in San Francisco brought a quick settlement by the mayor's emergency powers, and the cops did get a raise at the time. But public outrage over the strike led to several ballot measures that severely restricted police gains; the voters passed all of these by huge margins.

Police membership in such conglomerate labor unions as the Teamsters is particularly disturbing. Rather than establishing a basis for public respect for cops as professionals, such unions are more likely to homogenize police into the general labor mix. And recent allegations of serious, widespread corruption within the Teamsters Union make police participation in that organization ironic and incongruous at best, potentially corrupting or even criminal at worst.

Instead of accepting either unionized or civil service status, police must view themselves as professionals. No less important, the public and politicians must share this opinion and give police ample respect and remuneration. This change in attitude is crucial in our increasingly complex society, where cops make life-or-death decisions daily. We need the most sophisticated, professional persons possible to enforce our laws and protect our rights.

Yet almost nowhere is police work considered a profession, even though the cop's role in society is comparable to that of a doctor or lawyer in every way. Police have a specialized education, learn highly technical skills that require continual updating, and even speak a tailor-made language. Recently, too, police have been sued for "malpractice," a growing trend among dissatisfied citizens who deal with professionals in society.

Police work for the public good, prevent harm to citizens (or at least locate those guilty of harming others), uphold society's chosen regulations, and safeguard individual rights. Although cops may at times perform their duties imperfectly, that too may be characteristic of the other professions. The essential point is that police take an oath to protect all citizens, and for the most part they carry it off.

The historic social role of police is remarkably consistent with what they do today, a fact that I emphasize in my work with police departments. Unfortunately, most cops don't see themselves as professionals; understanding their own tradition as an elite service corps often helps change this impression.

The fact is that even the earliest societies had some form of police. Usually these men where chosen to guard the society's leaders—a tribal chieftain's warriors, an emperor's or king's guards. Ancient Greece had two distinct styles of law enforcement in its two principal city-states, Athens and Sparta. The Athenian democracy established and codified laws from earlier traditions; their special contributions to our own law enforcement ideals include humane treatment for law-breakers (even the notion of rehabilitation) and protection of the individual rights of citizens. Spartan law enforcement, like its society, took an opposite approach. There the police often operated in secret, gathering information about supposed traitors, who were likely to be punished or to just "disappear" from the community.

Both of these approaches to law enforcement were absorbed into the Roman Empire, where Caesar Augustus developed three separate divisions of police. From the military groups (the Centurians) he chose the Praetorian Guards and the Urban Cohorts. The Praetorian Guards were his personal bodyguards, comparable to our Secret Service. They inherited the Spartans' intelligence-gathering function, and their power was so great that they could impose or depose an emperor. (American society has experienced a similar growth of power in the law enforcement agencies surrounding the Presidency.) The Urban Cohorts existed to maintain peace and order in Rome—to quell riots and other disturbances. They were comparable to modern police tactical squads.

The third group of police, the Vigiles, were not military men. This force was organized into precincts across the city, and their duties were similar to those of today's beat cop—protecting citizens from crime and serving as agents of the judicial system. Crimes in Caesar's Rome were the same as the contemporary menaces, among them robbery, rape, murder, runaway children, family disputes. In addition to coping with the same problems as modern cops, the Vigiles had standard equipment that translates directly to the contemporary officer's arms: a short sword, which is comparable to the service revolver; a baton, which was the nightstick of its time; and leather thongs, which served the same purpose as handcuffs.

Police organization and functions went through many modifications on the European continent before the settling of the American colonies. Basically, the English pilgrims brought with them a tradition of common-law justice and the influence of the British sheriff and posse system of law enforcement. French settlers brought their constable system of police, and over time these influences merged and grew into modern American law enforcement.

Some police also existed among the original residents of North America. The Plains Indians, for example, had an elite group of men who organized and directed each tribe's food-gathering efforts. This practice was established not as a means of protecting the chief—as in many early societies—but in response to chaotic and unsuccessful hunting practices. Before hunts were organized, the tribe would approach a herd of buffalo from one side, running en masse at the usually docile animals. This practice often caused a stampede, and it almost never resulted in much meat for the tribe. So a few warriors were selected to police the hunt, and they in turn chose strong, swift men to encircle the herd and attack by surprise. When the Indians later got horses from Spanish settlers, these same police were in charge of the prized animals, with responsibility to dictate who could use them.

But truly modern police practices and policies had their foundation in Great Britain. In the late eighteenth century a reformer named Patrick Colquehoun published a treatise on the deficiencies and disorganization of London's seventy-odd police forces. The uproar caused by this and other cries for reform resulted in Home Secretary Robert Peel's proposal to Parliament, "An Act for Improving the Police in and near the Metropolis," which was passed in 1829. This comprehensive legislation established the four major tenets of police practice which form the basis for much of our modern law enforcement: 1) a clear definition of police authority; 2) qualifications for fitness of police, including provision for maintenance of fitness through education, training, and regular exercise; 3) a system of communication among police and storage of information helpful to police in their work (such as files on crimes and known criminals); 4) and a provision that each officer must wear a badge and identification number, and that each man should be responsible for his actions as a policeman—or be dismissed if he performed his duties improperly.

The effects of these nineteenth-century reforms are readily recognizable among police today, and they are basic to the profession of police work. Another long-established tradition—standards for height and weight—is on the way out, however. Minimum height for police officers is among the oldest provisions for these elite members of society, dating from Greek and Roman times when a ruler chose the biggest and strongest men to be his guards. The Roman Centurians literally stood a head above the rest of the population.

Such arbitrary standards are inappropriate for a modern society, where technological advantage can compensate for some cops' relatively small size. Moreover, such standards are discriminatory, and many law enforcement agencies have responded to this fact. Although a police officer must use physical agility and strength in performing certain functions, minimum height or maximum weight should not be the criteria for judging that officer's abilities. Rather, police training should include tests for strength and agility, and these skills should be retested at regular intervals throughout an officer's service in the department. If a cop cannot pass the physical tests, additional training should be provided, with a set period of time during which an officer must pass the tests or be removed from duty.

Most police with whom I have talked appreciate their tradition and recognize the need for continued reform in certain areas such as height standards. Many officers also are beginning to view their work as a service profession. Along with other professionals in service fields, police are almost universally motivated to help other people. They have consistently developed and upgraded the skills and training involved in their work. At times the improvements in law enforcement have been the result of outside pressures—from Peel's act of 1829 to the Sausalito council's establishment of psychiatric screening. Just as often the changes have come from within, perhaps in the form of better facilities and equipment requested by the officers or a big-city chief's ridding his department of corruption.

The impetus for professionalization has brought changes throughout many police departments. The educational level of police recruits is higher than ever; many rookie officers have college degrees, and many other police attend college part time to complete degrees or work on graduate studies. The content of aspiring police officers' studies also has increased in sophistication. For instance, many cops are going beyond introductory psychology to learn crisis intervention, behavioral motivation, specifics of drug and alcohol abuse, and other useful tools of social service. In fact, the young, well-educated officers entering police work today have changed my job somewhat—instead of offering fundamentals of self-knowledge and observation of other people's behavior, I am often called upon to discuss sophisticated questions of theory of motivation. This bodes well for the new breed of police officer.

Increased educational levels also tend to improve police performance, especially when personal discretion is involved. Generally, the better informed officers are about their own and others' behavior, the more capable they are of sound judgment in emergencies or tense situations. And the discretionary aspects of police authority are good indicators of a department's professional attitudes. Progressive police leaders encourage the exercise of individual discretion and provide training and counseling to help officers gain the necessary knowledge and confidence.

Police training likewise has become more complicated and sophisticated. Incredible though it sounds, the modern cop must learn some 3,000 individual skills to perform his duties. These skills include mastery of many different machines and weapons, all manner of paper work, thorough knowledge of local statutes and citizens' constitutional rights, familiarity with the various social services available to citizens, and much more. Of course changes in technology, laws, and bureaucratic red tape are routine, and police must update their skills continually. In-service training programs, seminars, and short courses at police academies help keep cops informed. A related aspect of police professionalization is a pay incentive program that many departments offer members who upgrade skills and continue their educations.

These improvements add up to careful screening of applicants and equally thorough training and supervision. We've seen plenty of examples of cops who weren't properly screened or trained—more than a third of the police in uniform today—and those persons perhaps have done the greatest disservice to police as a profession.

Because the public image of police has often been dominated by the bad cops—hostile, corrupt, violent, drunken—both politicians and ordinary citizens have a hard time viewing police as professionals. Then, too, the civilian is often a little afraid of cops, who represent authority and seemingly arbitrary force. Few people feel comfortable about police; most, if they were in trouble or saw someone else in trouble, would probably call the police, but would admit to being intimidated by cops. If most citizens know that the cops will assist them and preserve the basic structure of the society in which they enjoy many advantages, others—the less advantaged—may see police as their enemies, because the established order that cops support tends to keep the poor and powerless from making any substantial change in their status. And the desperate attempts of disadvantaged persons to change their lives are usually illegal—robbery, gambling, selling or using drugs, organizing militaristic groups to seize political power.

So the cop is the man in the middle. He must enforce laws and keep order in a society where many citizens hate him and others fear him. And at times, in the line of duty, the police officer must go against his own conscience and possibly arrest or discipline those with whom he sympathizes. The current wave of urban struggles over busing to achieve integrated schools is a good example of the conflicting loyalties facing police. The cops must quell the disturbances caused by racial tensions, an effort for which they usually earn only hatred and even sabotage by both blacks and whites. This is why police must be men and women whose strength and integrity will sustain them in the most difficult role in society.

The sheer difficulty of being a cop is one clear reason why police work should be considered a profession. But the mechanisms of government often work against this concept. Police today are officially designated as civil servants in virtually every community in the nation. Generally this status defines police as just another class of public employees who must fight for their slice of the municipal pie along with bus drivers and gardeners. Often, too, cops are governed by civil service regulations and standards that tend to protect mediocre workers and ignore innovative ones.

Yet the value of police to the community, as well as the particular need for healthy, stable individuals as cops, sets these people apart from other public employees. Police should not be lumped together with all other municipal workers, nor should bad cops be protected by the formal or informal tenure system of civil service. More important, applicants for police work should be screened and tested for their specific functions, not chosen from some general listing of civil service aspirants. And police should be paid like professionals. Their combination of education, training, and enormous responsibility should be adequately compensated—with a full measure of public respect to go with it. In short, we should recognize and reward the special nature of police work and the men and women willing and able to do it.

12

A Private Session

AN OFFICER who is psychologically unsuited for police work can perform adequately for years without showing signs of a bad cop. Eventually, however, the pressures will get to him and he will respond in negative ways. In this case, after eight years as a police officer, Bob V. began to step out on his wife, Barbara, and when she protested, he beat her. This was the first time he had ever exhibited anger in this way—in fact he had always thought of himself as a good-humored person "with a long, long fuse." But one day he drew his service revolver and threatened a man who (he thought) wanted to run away with Barbara. This action might have constituted grounds for immediate dismissal, but the chief of Bob's department knew that cases like this happen all the time—to both good and bad cops—so before acting he demanded that Bob see me. The following is a portion of one of our interviews—it is specific to Bob V.'s case, but it represents many hundreds of interviews that I have had with police officers with similar problems:

Shev: Who did you talk to, the chief or the captain?

Bob: Both.

Shev: I haven't talked with them. What did they tell you?

Bob: Just that if you thought it was all right for me to go back to work, they would go along with that. I can start again on Saturday. Basically what it is, if there are any screw-ups whatsoever involving my marital problems or anything, it'll be all over. I'll be fired.

Shev: How do you feel about that?

Bob: Well, I can understand their point, to a degree. It depends. In other words, if I go home and have a beef with my wife and she goes down to the department screaming about it and I get canned, I'd feel kind of shitty about it.

Shev: You mean you're afraid she might blackmail you now when she knows about this?

Bob: You know she went down to the station before. She holds it over my head: "Either you be a good boy or else I'll talk to your captain about it." So it could happen. I don't think it will, but it could happen. I have to be very careful about what I do or say around the house, just to get along.

Shev: Has she filed for a divorce yet—dissolution?

Bob: Yes, she's filed.

Shev: And how are the children reacting to this?

Bob: I don't think they really understand.

Shev: I realize they're confused, but how are they reacting to this confusion?

Bob: Well, I don't know. Things are different for them, and their biggest concern right now is why their mother's not home with them right now. That's the big thing right now. I don't think—they don't realize that in a very short time they're going to be moving and I'm not going to be around any longer.

Shev: You can cry. It's perfectly all right. Why shouldn't you cry? Why are you trying to keep from crying?

Bob: I'm tired of it.

Shev: Because it makes you so angry?

Bob: Yeah, it makes me angry.

Shev: How do you feel about these kids?

Bob: I don't know how to answer that, you know. They mean an awful lot to me, you know. They mean a lot to me.

Shev: Yes, I realize that.

Bob: I don't want to lose them.

Shev: But do you have to lose them?

Bob: Yeah.

Shev: Why do you have to lose them?

Bob: I don't uh—why do I *have* to lose them? Because they're being taken away from me. They're not going to be there anymore.

Shev: But aren't you going to have visitation rights and things of that sort?

Bob: I don't know yet, to be quite honest with you.

Shev: Why not?

Bob: Well, I can't picture myself being a weekend father. Or to call for an appointment to see your kids.

Shev: Does this have any memories for you from the past?

Bob: Not really. Because there was nothing like this in the past.

Shev: I mean your own past.

Bob: Yeah, I know what you're talking about. There was never anything like this in my own past.

Shev: What was your past like, I mean the circumstances?

Bob: Well, you see, I didn't know anything like this. I was very young, you know. I grew up—.

Shev: How old were you?

Bob: Six months.

Shev: Six months?

Bob: Yeah, so I'm told. You see, I don't even know that. I don't know anything about it. The only thing I know is I was raised by my grandmother and I got along *very well* with her and everything was fine and dandy. There was never any question in my mind as to why I was there or anything else that I can recall at this time. It was a natural thing that she was raising me, that I lived with her. That was the natural thing to me because that is the only thing I'd ever known.

Shev: Yes, but your father would come back, you said last time.

Bob: He'd come back every year, maybe every other year, something like that.

Shev: When he arrived, what was your feeling, do you remember?

Bob: Yeah, it was just like it would be if an aunt or uncle would come. I mean, that's your uncle, that's your dad. OK. Fine. You accept that. It wasn't the same. My grandmother was my parents. She *was* my parents. My father was somebody else. He was an acquaintance—.

Shev: Didn't you ever cry at night and wish your father were there with you?

Bob: No. Never did.

Shev: In other words, you never allowed yourself to feel this way?

Bob: I think at that age, I don't think I was really concerned about allowing myself or not. I wasn't interested in it, you know.

Shev: OK. Let me explain something to you—a trick of the mind. May I?

Bob: Sure.

Shev: You see, you've got to have wished you'd had a father. Every child does. Boy or girl. You got a mother, we'll call your grandmother your mother, OK? So you've got to have wished you had a father, because the other kids had fathers. Now you may have played a trick on yourself, and said to yourself, I'm not going to think about not having a father, or I know I've got a father and he's off in Washington doing something great. Do you understand how kids fantasize these things?

Bob: Yeah, I can understand.

Shev: But what you did, apparently, was pretend you didn't have a father, and you were angry to the point of suppressing it and saying I will not even think about it. Now, a person who does this at your age, six months to five years, isn't going to be consciously aware of what they're doing. So now today when we talk about it, you say to me very honestly, "Lookit, I can't ever remember wishing I had a father," or words to that effect. Do you understand what I'm saying?

Shev: What I'm trying to get across to you is you have deluded yourself all these years, which is one of the cornerstones of your anger and your depression, which I picked up the first time you came in to see me.

Bob: Can't really buy that.

Shev: I'm not asking you to buy it. I want you to think about it.

Bob: But the point is that I *was* honest with you. If I'd come in that same room and said I'd led a normal childhood life with a father and a mother and never been any orphan, no one would ever have been the wiser. You're looking at things I told you and making something out of it. I really believe that. I mean if I had laid down a good foundation, the happy background and no hangups, I don't think you'd have been any the wiser right then, not after a one-hour confrontation.

Shev: Keep talking.

Bob: Just what I'm saying. I don't think you can really honestly believe that in one hour you can make that kind of prediction that I've got all of these hangups because of my father, other than going back on what you've seen in the past or what you know should be the problems because it says so here or there or whatever.

Shev: Don't you think you just got through answering your own doubts as to why I knew?

Bob: Why? Because it says so in some textbook? Right

down the line? That's the way it should be?

Shev: You've been in police work how long?

Bob: Eight years.

Shev: And when you go to a crime and you investigate it, you find that crimes have a way of being repetitive, don't they?

Bob: Right. And you accept things on face value to begin with. That's what you're saying.

Shev: The modus operandi of a person involved in crime is going to be repetitive, isn't it?

Bob: To a degree, yeah.

Shev: Why is that, do you know?

Bob: Because of the individual.

Shev: Yes. And why is that individual operating that way?

Bob: Because it's him, that's the way he operates.

Shev: But you see, a certain group of people who think that way and operate that way are always going to operate in that direction. That modus operandi is going to be true not just of one individual, but of a whole series of individuals.

Bob: The same modus operandi?

Shev: Yeah.

Bob: Not necessarily so. I don't think so.

Shev: You haven't been around police work all that long. You haven't got a good background.

Bob: I think I've got a fantastic background.

Shev: You're not being honest with me, are you?

Bob: Yeah, I am. You're talking about modus operandi, and it depends on what you're talking about. I think maybe you might have lost me as to how you're trying to read that. I fail to see it.

Shev: I wonder why you don't want to see it.

Bob: I don't think that has anything to do with it. You're talking about a group that is going to have the same modus operandi. Are you talking about a group of individuals from various places? I don't know what you're saying. I don't—

hell—there's a lot of people that would do that. I mean that's what modus operandi is all about, is to make one person different from somebody else.

Shev: But what we're talking about is five or six guys using the same modus operandi who have no relationship to each other.

Bob: Yeah, but it won't be the same throughout. They'll be different.

Shev: But the general behavior is going to be the same.

Bob: OK.

Shev: Now, how do you suppose this is accomplished by these guys who have never known each other, never talked to one another?

Bob: Well, I don't know. Armed robbers, they usually use guns, too.

Shev: You're changing the subject.

Bob: No, no.

Shev: Yes, you are. We're talking about a broader thing here. I don't blame you for resisting.

Bob: I don't mean to resist. I'm just trying to get straight just what you're after.

Shev: You see, these individual guys that operate similarly in a crime pattern have had similar psychiatric programming, from birth to five years of age. If you go into their background, you find that they have similar backgrounds, and from this you can postulate how they're going to operate, in terms of their psychic response. Now, if you had come in here and lied to me about your background, it would have come through loud and clear: this man is lying to me.

Bob: Am I lying now?

Shev: No. But you're not also telling me the truth either.

Bob: Now what does that mean?

Shev: Just that.

Bob: I'm not lying, but I'm not telling the truth?

Shev: That's right, you're not.

Bob: What am I doing then?

Shev: You're fencing with me. Because you feel you're here under duress.

Bob: Yes and no, I guess.

Shev: You just told me at the beginning the chief said to you "Look, you can come back to work as long as you continue treatment." You have resistance anyway about coming here because you don't like to admit that you over-reacted and overresponded. You don't like to admit that you made a fool out of yourself with Barbara. You can't even get angry at me, and I've been provoking you and I've been pushing you.

Bob: Why is that, Doctor, if I'm a very angry person?

Shev: The angriest people I know very seldom express their anger. Bob, before we get back to this, let me say something. I can't tell everything about you from one interview.

Bob: I know.

Shev: That's true. But with my knowledge and skills, I can give one hell of a close prognostication.

Bob: If you're getting the level from the person you're interviewing.

Shev: If I don't get it, it comes out somewhere along the line, too, and that's exactly what I'd record. You know how many guys come in here and lie to me about themselves?

Bob: Probably 90 per cent.

Shev: That's right. Maybe more. And do you know the thing they lie to me about the most?

Bob: I would take a rough guess and say probably sex.

Shev: Sex and their wives. And how they get along with them. And what is the second area they lie to me about the most? Their parents and themselves.

Bob: Are they actually lying or are they just letting it slide off because they don't really care?

Shev: Oh, they care all right. Everybody cares about their parents.

Bob: Does it make me wrong if I don't?

Shev: That doesn't make you wrong. In this business we don't have rights and wrongs, remember? Let's pretend that you're me and you have to listen to your own story. How would you go about it?

Bob: With my story?

Shev: Your history.

Bob: Well, to begin with, I wouldn't even want to hear it. I mean, that was the first thing we hit on. Boom. Let's go back to when you were a little kid. That's a stereotype of a psychiatrist, right there. You see it all the time. Why do you hate your mother? As far as I'm concerned, it's unreal. I think you're digging up a problem, if you want to call it that. It's over and done with, a long time ago, and really has no bearings on any of my feelings right now. Period. And I could care less about—.

Shev: Then what are you angry about?

Bob: I'm angry at my present situation. Now.

Shev: How did you get into your situation?

Bob: It didn't start when I was five years old, two years old, or whatever.

Shev: You're sure of that?

Bob: Yeah.

Shev: You don't see any similarities between your relationship to Barbara and your reasons for wanting to stay married to her, and the past?

Bob: None whatsoever.

Shev: The entire past from birth on.

Bob: Not at that age. I don't know how you can say it had any bearing when I'm not even conscious of it. I'm not guided by my subconscious thoughts, thoughts I don't even know are there, those aren't the ones that guide me.

Shev: Are you sure about that?

Bob: Yes.

Shev: How can you be that certain?

Bob: If you tell me to do something, and I don't hear you

tell me to do it, it's not going to do any good for you to say it, right? If I have some thoughts I'm not even aware I have, then, well, they're not doing anything, if I don't know I've got those thoughts, what good are they? It's the same as not being there, and maybe they're *not* even there.

Shev: Go on.

Bob: That's all I have to say, I guess.

Shev: You know, I do feel sorry for you, Bob, I really do.

Bob: Thanks.

Shev: You know why?

Bob: Why?

Shev: Constant protestation. Interferes with your thinking. You know what we've been talking about is the truth, and you're frightened of it. You see, Bob, when you say you can't remember, or why should something from your childhood influence your thinking today, people have asked that question for a million years before Dr. Freud came along and was able to put the pieces together and point out how that works. And of course everybody—.

Bob: His *theory* of how that works.

Shev: Yes, and everybody in the modern world knows that he was right. Everybody can see that.

Bob: Well, how come there are so many different thinkings along these lines?

Shev: There is no division of thinking on that one point.

Bob: On Freud?

Shev: On that one point that the unconscious controls our motivation behavior. What people do disagree on is how much influence, and what direction, and at what point. But no one ever disagrees on the basic point. Now, I think you have to get back to something. Your marrying of Barbara wasn't pure accident. Your miserable life with her wasn't pure accident either.

Bob: Didn't have a miserable life.

Shev: Yes, you did. You told me you did.

Bob: There were times that were miserable, but there were also a lot of good times.

Shev: What are you crying about?

Bob: Nothing.

Shev: Nothing? How much do you dislike yourself when you cry like this?

Bob: (strained laugh)

Shev: Because you don't want to cry do you?

Bob: Jesus.

Shev: And you're awfully confused, aren't you?

Bob: That's what they tell me.

Shev: By the way, did you do what I asked you to do—to write those vignettes about the important people in your childhood?

Bob: Yeah, but I forgot them.

Shev: How come?

Bob: Because there was a family hassle this morning.

Shev: Tell me about the family hassle.

Bob: I got up, told Barbara I had to have the car today because I was coming over here.

Shev: What happened?

Bob: It flipped her off.

Shev: What did she say?

Bob: She came unglued about—oh, Christ—about having to drive the truck and I knew it and should have made other arrangements—and I don't know.

Shev: What did you say?

Bob: I didn't say anything; I got up, got dressed and left. I had said it all to her before.

Shev: What are you thinking.

Bob: What am I thinking?

Shev: Yeah.

Bob: I'm beginning to feel like a damn nut being over here.

Shev: That's good. Maybe we're getting to you.

Bob: What?

Shev: Maybe it's good for you to talk.

Bob: I don't have anything to say.

Shev: How angry did she make you this morning?

Bob: Not really—she was angry—but I expected it. Didn't really bother me.

Shev: Is she going out with other men?

Bob: I don't think so.

Shev: How long do you think it's been since she hasn't liked you?

Bob: I don't know.

Shev: Why is she so angry with you?

Bob: She says because I beat her.

Shev: Is that the first time you ever beat her? The only time? Didn't she used to make you furious?

Bob: I don't know what I did.

Shev: You just stepped out on her. Because you shut up and didn't talk to her. How would you handle your anger toward her?

Bob: How would I know?

Shev: Then, in the past.

Bob: We'd usually make up during the argument. It never carried over. We never had any long-standing grudge or argument.

Shev: Bob, you stepped out on her and I think we sort of both agree it was because you had an unconscious anger toward her. She wasn't warm and sexually accepting of you.

Bob: Yeah.

Shev: And that was consistent in your marriage, from what you tell me.

Bob: Uh, yes and no. No, it wasn't consistent. There were times, but—.

Shev: What are you thinking now?

Bob: I was thinking about some things Barb had said.

Shev: What did she say?

Bob: She was joking with one of her girl friends the other night. It got around to leaving me and it was a big joke to them . . . why should she . . . they don't need anything . . . big joke.

Shev: Maybe she sees something about you, that you're a little bit hurt by this?

Bob: Probably.

Shev: Maybe it's sort of a trial balloon. You don't feel you deserve anything—.

Bob: Who doesn't?

Shev: You.

Bob: Well, shit, I feel I deserve it all, every bit of it.

Shev: The good and the bad?

Bob: No, I'm not talking about the bad. I've got enough of that already.

Shev: How many men in the department know that you come to see me?

Bob: Knowing the police department, probably everybody. You never tell anybody not to tell anybody, so policemen like to gossip.

Shev: How do you feel about it, their knowing you're coming here?

Bob: Couldn't care less.

Shev: Couldn't care less? You remind me of the little boy going past the cemetery, and he's scared shitless, but he's saying "I'm not scared. Watch me, I'm whistling." (Shev makes obscene noise)

Bob: (laughs)

Shev: Did that have any meaning for you?

Bob: What you just did?

Shev: Nah. I don't give a shit. Not me. You know what I'm going to say to you?

Bob: You don't have to say—.

Shev: I'm going to quote an old Nebraska farmer. "Bullshit." That you understand.

Bob: Yeah.

Shev: You going to bring those little vignettes with you next Monday?

Bob: I will, but I don't know why you want them, anyway.

Shev: That's all right. You put down what you think I want, all right?

Bob's marriage ended in divorce soon afterward. Although he married again within a year, his second marriage soon began to show the same weaknesses as the first—lack of communication, an air of distrust, violent arguments, accusations, beatings. Today Bob works for a different police department and is drinking heavily, often while on duty. But it is doubtful—basically because of stringent civil service requirements—that he will ever be dismissed. To my mind he has become the classic example of the bad cop: the anger he could never believe had been smoldering inside him is now unexpectedly and suddenly released against the citizens he is supposed to serve. And because he cannot bring himself to consider why and how the anger got there in the first place, he will never be able to keep it under control. Someday he may draw that service revolver on an innocent person and use it.

The tragic fact about police today is that *many* experience similar personal problems but do not receive any help at all. About 50 per cent of this group continue to assault their wives (and children), and 10 to 20 per cent of those will either kill or be killed by family members. A higher percentage will end up committing suicide. The chief and captain of a department may see this happening, but because of the protections of civil service requirements or other forms of seniority systems, they will be able to do little more than issue a reproach.

13
Cops and Crime

No MATTER HOW well police officers respond to calls and investigate complaints, a police department's value to its community also depends on the judgment of individual officers and the policies of the chief. That is, the *way* the police enforce the laws may be as important as the laws themselves or the extent to which those laws are enforced.

This is a subtle area in police work, mostly a matter of attitude on the part of cops. And because at least 80 per cent of a policeman's work is providing service to citizens—handling traffic control, answering questions, calming frightened citizens—the cop's point of view is paramount. The objective I've worked for in counseling and instructing police is a flexible, *helpful* attitude that expresses the officer's concern but does not get him emotionally involved in the situation. If police can achieve such an attitude, they will also be able to remain calm and objective when faced with infractions of the law or emergencies that require quick, decisive action. The cop who is professional and relaxed, for example, won't react hostilely or punitively to a driver who has made a wrong turn or a kid who is autographing store windows with shaving cream.

Similarly, a chief's preference for strict enforcement or for pragmatic, conscientious community service can set the tone for the entire department. If the chief is moralistic and rather narrow-minded in his interpretation of ordinances or unwritten public constraints, he can rule a police force that allows minimal freedom of expression (no matter what state or federal laws or even the Constitution guarantees). But if a chief's attitude is flexible yet practical, his department can provide full services and protection to the community without infringing on anyone's personal freedoms. Such a chief is also likely to encourage his officers to use discretion in interpreting situations, rather than feel compelled to arrest citizens or give citations for every possible infraction.

Nowhere in the law enforcement field can the individual police officer bring more positive influence than in the area of juvenile offenses. Indeed, police handling of juvenile offenders encompasses all the subtle aspects of this work—attitude, understanding, discretion, empathy. Cops usually care about youngsters and enjoy helping them more than do other citizens, but unfortunately, the laws of most communities offer few alternatives to arrest and prosecution of juveniles. Social services that should support any law enforcement team are often inadequate or nonexistent.

Some communities have tried to improve this situation, though, including at least two departments for which I have consulted. When Ed Kreins left Sausalito as chief, he moved to a city where 60 per cent of the population was under eighteen. One of Kreins's first programs was establishment of the Youth Services Bureau, a division that incorporated both police officers and a variety of counselors and paraprofessionals. My role as consultant to the Bureau was similar to that for the department at large: I gave lectures to the officers and counselors assigned to the Bureau on subjects related to their work, such as adolescent rebellion, drug use and its effects among young persons, family dynamics, and basic psychological development. In addition, I worked with individual counselors and officers, discussing their duties and adding my professional perspective to their training and experience.

The Bureau's staff performs a wide range of services for young people, including a school liaison program; safety instruction for bicyclists, hunters, and school traffic monitors; a speakers' bureau and public awareness program; parent involvement groups; and a program in which young persons over age fourteen (and adults) can ride along with police on patrol. These efforts have been rewarded by a significant decrease in young persons' involvements in crime or, if previously arrested, repeated offenses. Both youngsters and adult residents of this city have responded enthusiastically to the Bureau's programs, reporting that they find the local police to be "human beings"; "courteous"; "friendly"; and "youth-oriented."

In working with police in all departments—whether or not they are assigned to the juvenile bureau—I encourage the same flexible attitude toward young persons that a healthy cop should have toward all citizens. One means I use is to get each officer to recall the experiences and adult models that influenced him to go into police work. As is explained in Chapter 5, many police have been reared in homes where the parental models are incomplete or absent, and someone has filled an influential role—a teacher, coach, minister, family doctor. If a cop can recognize that he in turn may provide the same example for the young persons whom he meets in his work, his authority can become a positive influence on juvenile offenders.

The old-fashioned cop might choose to use his authority as a deterrent. For example, one officer recalled that he had been in trouble as a teenager and that the local cops' strict treatment had intimidated him into changing his habits.

When this officer was called by a store owner to pick up a boy who had been caught shoplifting, the cop went through the whole police procedure: he asked the boy for identification, which the youngster didn't have; he handcuffed the boy and took him to the station; he had him booked and placed alone in a holding cell for half an hour, with no opportunity to contact his family or anyone else. In the meantime the officer telephoned the youth's parents, explaining that he was going to put a scare into the boy so that he'd think twice about stealing anything in the future. The parents approved this action and agreed to act as if they had not talked to the officer. After the youngster had had plenty of time to ponder his fate, the cop removed him from the cell, had him phone his parents, then sternly warned the boy that any further trouble with the police would mean jail—no questions asked. The kid got the message; he has not been in trouble since.

Effective as it might be, this sort of treatment is extremely negative—it succeeds only by scaring the youngster rather than teaching him respect for law and the rights of others. Indeed, many cops today shun such a traditional application of authority. More typical of well-educated police officers is the innovative use of their authority as a means of psychological impact. One officer in the Youth Services Bureau wanted to discuss a juvenile's problems with his parents. But repeated phone calls and letters to these parents brought no response, so one evening the officer phoned the parents and informed them that the next night he would come to their home and officially take them to police headquarters to question them about their son's offenses. The parents must have thought the cop was bluffing, for they rejected another chance to go in on their own. So the next evening that officer did make his "arrests," and gradually he even got cooperation from this family.

Another juvenile officer had no difficulty meeting with one boy's parents, but the couple seemed unconcerned that their son had repeatedly been in trouble with the police. After several unproductive discussions with these parents—each time after some new incident involving the boy—the officer sat down with the juvenile and his parents for one more conference. He looked straight at the couple and said, "I'd like to recommend some psychological counseling in this situation." Before anyone could comment or object, the cop continued: "You're the ones who need the treatment, because your child is a reflection of you." That officer's assertion had the right effect—both parents and son went into family therapy, with promising results for all concerned.

In certain other areas, an officer's personal attitudes or prejudices can result in unequal treatment of varying groups of citizens. Some form of racial prejudice has touched all of us, and cops are no exception. Because the majority of police are white, and because probably half of all urban crimes are committed by members of minority groups, there is often a sentiment among police that blacks, Chicanos, or Puerto Ricans are likely suspects for whatever crimes occur. This prejudice can lead individual officers to treat minority citizens with less respect than they give other people, mentally making suspects of all minority persons and criminals of all minority suspects. The well-educated, healthy police officer, on the other hand, is aware of his prejudice and is not influenced by his knowledge of crime statistics when dealing with any particular group of citizens. Again, the chief's attitude can be crucial: if his policy strictly prohibits mistreatment of any citizen, the officer whose prejudice is uncontrolled will be obvious, and that person will be subject to disciplinary action or dismissal.

Another sensitive subject among police is their contacts with and feelings about homosexuals. Particularly in major urban areas, police must deal with gay men and women, usually in routine matters, but sometimes while enforcing the law. Because of confusion about their own sexual identity or unconscious fears that they may be homosexuals themselves, many cops react with hostility or even violence when confronted with members of the gay community. Such attitudes are often compounded by a strong prejudice against anyone whose behavior deviates from narrowly defined norms. Only education and increased self-awareness can dispel these notions. Some departments have made important strides in this area, notably in San Francisco, where police relations with the homosexual residents are generally restrained and cordial.

To maintain his professionalism and flexibility a cop must first understand himself and his personal hangups, but he also can benefit from an understanding of the dynamics of others' personalities and problems. For example, police often come in contact with drug addicts or pushers, although they may not be able to arrest them or assist in a successful prosecution. This alone is a source of frustration for most cops, and their reaction to such persons may be overly hostile or abusive. Yet a policeman must realize that the drug addict usually can't help himself: he is acting out a deep-seated compulsion, rather than some evil design or rebellion against society. As in many other situations, the "criminal" needs help more than punishment.

Although it's never easy for a group of police to view a drug pusher sympathetically, I point out to them that the pusher may sincerely believe that he's doing a service. His "clients" are people like himself—usually addicts—and he is simply their current supplier. Especially in light of the increasing popularity of marijuana and cocaine, police must realize that many law-abiding citizens are beginning to regard dealers and pushers as useful business people.

This is not to say that selling drugs is an acceptable social act, but I emphasize to cops that by understanding at least part of the complex motivation behind the pusher's role they can act dispassionately and avoid overzealous errors as breaking into the homes of innocent people or brutalizing suspects.

In some areas of law enforcement, education or understanding is not sufficient, however. Many cops' attitudes about issues of morality and personal freedom (usually in relation to sexual behavior) need to be reformed. Police must be educated to realize that they are not the arbiters or initiators of the community's moral standards: rather, they are charged with upholding the laws and limitations that result from citizens' consensus. This view often is very difficult for a chief or individual officer to accept, because his own beliefs may be more strict than the community's laws.

There are areas, however, where society forces the police to assume the role of arbiter of morality, and this is potentially very dangerous. In many large cities, for example, prostitutes and panhandlers are allowed to ply their trades until at some vague and undetermined point they are declared "out of hand" by the press or by outraged citizens. At this point the police are blamed for letting the situation spread beyond control; yet if they "crack down on the hookers and the beggars" as the headlines demand, they are maligned by liberal groups as wasting their time with "victimless crimes" and not concentrating on "real crimes" of assault, robbery, and so forth. When things settle down again the police are faced with the problem of "keeping the lid on" prostitution and panhandling, which leads to the sort of incident where a prostitute on one side of the street is arrested while a prostitute on the other side of the street is allowed to continue soliciting.

The same problem applies to chronic alcoholics and drug addicts on "skid row" and to pornographic bookshop and theater owners. We cannot allow the police to pick and choose areas of law enforcement while we as a society try to make up our minds: not only do we diffuse the power of the laws that we do want enforced, we also pave the way for pernicious criminal elements that make the situation worse than ever. Pimps who brutally abuse and virtually imprison the prostitutes of certain neighborhoods; criminals in the "protection" racket who strong-arm their way into receiving payoffs from pornographic booksellers and theater owners; and high-powered drug dealers who exploit and perpetuate the wretched condition of drug addicts are all the result of the intolerable indifference of society about the way its laws are enforced.

Many of these problems could be resolved if we stopped averting our eyes from uncomfortable situations and owned up to our responsibility as a civilized people. Prostitution, for example, has existed and will continue to exist whether or not we pass laws against it. In today's society, police could be more even-handed if they adopted a laissez faire attitude about prostitution and involved themselves only when a crime occurred, such as robbery, vagrancy, creating a nuisance, pickpocketing, or assault.

In all instances, the police must provide equal protection under the law. Citizens—including pornographic theater owners and booksellers—must have enough confidence in the police to report criminal activities. Yet, because of the public's unfavorable attitude toward businesses that deal in pornographic materials and the general unfriendliness of police toward such operations, these small business operators often have no effective protection from unwanted "partners" or violent scare tactics.

What we should *not* require the police to do—and unfortunately most cities do give this function to their police departments—is to handle the licensing of businesses, taxi drivers, news reporters, and entertainment establishments. This is an administrative responsibility which could be better provided by the city clerk or assistant to the city council. It imposes a burden of paper work and fee collection on highly trained police and gives them a regulatory power that may conflict with the community's laws or citizen's rights, including that of free enterprise. For instance, police licensing power may serve to restrain competition among taxicab companies by giving favored treatment to one or two firms. Similarly, city ordinances may not prohibit showing of pornographic films or opening a massage parlor, but the police chief or his subordinates might choose to deny such businesses the right to operate. This is not a police prerogative—only the law-making body of the community can write the laws, and the police should not be involved unless there is a question of legality. One means of resolving this problem is to have one city agency handle license applications and collect fees, while a police information bureau could be assigned to conduct routine background checks on applicants before their licenses are granted. In this way a potential business operator who does not meet legal qualifications could be identified, but the police would not be in the role of licensing agents.

Perhaps the area most in need of new controls is the policy of many departments that allows police to carry guns off duty. In California and other states, *retired* peace officers can own and even carry their service revolvers, a policy that is patently ridiculous. Retirement is the standard method of getting a cop with problems off the force, whether he is someone whose emotional burdens make him unable to perform his duties, someone whose drinking has become too blatant to be covered up by him or his friends, or someone whose treatment of suspects is so brutal as to make him a liability to the department. (Of course many other police could be described in this way, but as yet they haven't been taken out of uniform.) So the state law sanctions the people who've washed out as police to carry the guns that they should never have been given. This law must be changed; such efforts in many state legislatures to date have failed.

Furthermore, working police should not carry guns when

off duty: a proposal for guns to be kept at the police station for use only when necessary should be adopted in all communities. The London bobbies are often cited as examples of police not carrying guns at all, when in fact most other British police (detectives, special details, riot control units) do carry guns when on duty. But all weapons are stored at the police stations in Britain, for use only by officers on duty; bobbies are given weapons if they are in dangerous situations (such as a terrorist seige or a shoot-out of some kind). Such a policy is sound and effective for British police, and it could drastically reduce the number of deaths associated with off-duty police in this country. Approximately 150 persons are killed by off-duty cops each year in the United States, most of them in situations that do not involve a crime but rather such incidents as a drunken cop shooting his gun off in a bar or a policeman's gun discharging "accidentally."

Both changes in policy toward carrying guns—removing the retired officer's authority to carry a gun and issuing weapons only to on-duty cops—are matters of great controversy. Many public officials, citizens' groups, and police associations strongly oppose any change in current attitudes or policies, and they cite statistics telling how many lives are saved or criminals apprehended by armed off-duty cops. Other groups support experiments in limiting police access to and use of guns, and some departments have adopted policies by which officers may fire only in defense of their own or other citizens' lives.

But this controversy—like most others surrounding the actions of police on or off duty—is a smoke screen that obscures the real issues. If our methods of selecting police recruits were thorough and professional to begin with, if we trained them properly, if we defined their role in society more clearly, and if we helped them to understand and cope with the sometimes intolerable pressures of their daily work, we would very rarely have to deal with the outrageous action of off-duty cops discharging guns in a bar. The healthy, well-educated cop who views his work as a service to society can be the strongest deterrent to misuse of police weapons.

14
Cops and Their Future

THE TRADITIONAL image of the law enforcement officer in American history is that of a Matt Dillon type—the six-foot, four-inch marshal who keeps the peace by the power of his gun or fists. So entrenched is this image in all phases of our society that only recently have we even considered withdrawing height and sex limitations from the requirements for police service. It is time to reassess our understanding of what the police are supposed to do, and the kind of people we want to select as police. Until we do this, our society will continue to be subjected to the arbitrary abuses of the bad cop.

What does any society expect from its police force? Most people believe the cops are there to protect life and property, or to fight crime, or to keep the peace. All these answers only hint at the real function of police, however, which is to preserve the established order. In a democracy, this order is a system of laws and regulations that we as a society elect to maintain. The police, then, represent us collectively, but they enforce these laws individually—and it is on the personal level, in the day-to-day routine of a beat or patrol, that the American system is tested in far more important ways than during sensational "headline eras" such as the violent sixties or the crime-ridden seventies. And it is there that the individual judgment of the average cop carries much more weight than his nightstick or gun.

Take away Matt Dillon's size and his guns and he remains a flexible, educable, intelligent human being who uses force only as a last resort and has deep respect for the law and the people he serves. For it is the officer's attitude toward himself and the people he deals with that makes the law meaningful—negatively or positively—to the average citizen. This is a huge burden to place on anyone's shoulders, but as I have suggested, the good cop is the very person who wants to carry it. His motivation is to "rescue" people—not by punishing them (which is a bad cop's form of rescue), but by helping them out of troubled situations. A friendly gesture, a kind remark, a soothing, calm demeanor that can help people cope with everyday problems—this is the good cop's best compensation, even when he is in the midst of a difficult arrest or an ugly family brawl.

No cop can function well, however, if a third of his colleagues are psychologically unsuited for police work and endanger or corrupt his best efforts. And no good cop, no matter how much of a "natural" he is, can withstand the many pressures of police work alone. He must have a proper outlet where he can unload the pressures of the day and a way to learn more about himself and about the behavior of the people he serves, arrests, tickets, reprimands, counsels. Even some of the more progressive attempts to help police and their families cope with pressures—such as allowing wives to ride with their husbands on patrol—do not provide a continuing program where deeper questions can be confronted and discussed with the help of a skilled psychiatrist. And since many of these questions begin unconsciously and are only brought to the surface in the midst of a no-holds-barred group discussion, such an ongoing forum is vital.

Unfortunately, psychiatric in-service programs currently in operation are few. And yet it would be so simple and so inexpensive to do it. One psychiatrist can effectively handle the in-service program for a department of more than 150 men by spending only twelve to twenty-four hours a month on *all* phases of the program. (It is the *continuous* exposure over a long period of time that counts, not the number of hours spent in a bull session or screening interview at any one time.) If the department has 300 men, two psychiatrists can handle the program; if 1500 men, ten psychiatrists—it's just that simple.

The police psychiatrists should charge their usual hourly fee, which, even if $100 per hour, only adds up to $1200 to $2400 per month—a small price to pay for keeping good cops healthy and bad cops out.

A significant first step has been made in the New York Police Department, where a psychological counseling unit provides troubled officers with evaluations, light counseling, and referrals to specialists in alcoholism, marital relations, debt management, and emotional problems. Headed by a Ph.D. in clinical psychology who is himself a patrolman, the staff of eleven counselors is comprised of other police officers who hold master's degrees in psychology and are working on their doctorates. This program could easily and inexpensively be expanded to include consulting psychiatrists and psychologists who are *not* connected with the department and who are brought in to screen recruits, set up weekly bull sessions, and provide individual counseling to officers and their spouses.

Communities that anticipate starting a psychiatric program would benefit by going beyond the practices I've developed, by establishing standards that are more rigorous than any in use at present. For example, in the cities and states where I consult with police, my assessment of an applicant is merely a recommendation to the chief, who has final authority to hire. I believe, however, that the psychiatric assessment of each applicant should outweigh the personal or political pressures on a chief. This would result in fewer mistakes in hiring cops, and it would allow the chief to counter the pressures that politicians, citizens, or other cops often place on him to hire their friends or relatives.

The application and screening process could definitely be improved, starting with a new requirement that all applicants must have at least two years of a liberal arts education. Each candidate should be interviewed on at least two separate occasions so that the psychiatrist could follow up on topics discussed in the first meeting. This policy also seems more fair to an applicant who might be extremely nervous in an unfamiliar situation—the second interview would be a known quantity.

But the psychiatric evaluation should not stop there. Once hired, the recruit should become a cadet for two years, during which he would serve a year-long, rotating apprenticeship in a neighboring department where he would learn all police functions. After the apprentice year, the cadet would then reapply to the department he had originally chosen, and further personal and psychiatric evaluation would be made. Once hired he would be placed on probationary status for a full two years, at the end of which he would again be interviewed by a psychiatrist and made a permanent employee. I cannot overemphasize the importance of this probationary period: for borderline cops—even for some who on the surface seem to have all the qualities of a good cop—it may take all of two years for accumulating pressures to bring out the kind of reactions that signal deeper characteristics of the bad cop. Unfortunately, the probationary status in most departments today ranges from only one month to one year. Often it is attached to civil service requirements and thus becomes a formality at best.

Again, assessment of the officer's performance should not

stop after he has passed the probationary period. Regardless of its size, complexity, or orientation, every department should have a continuing mechanism to determine the quality of its police officers—through yearly evaluation and testing, for example. If an officer is found wanting, he should be demoted or fired, although he should always have a right to appeal to a review board or citizens' committee.

Another means of checking performance is through complaints from the public. These should not be handled by a desk sergeant but by a captain or someone who ranks above him. This practice keeps high-level officers in touch with the public and aware of their subordinates' weaknesses (or alleged weaknesses). A captain's attention to complaints may in itself calm angry citizens, so long as he follows through with an investigation and appropriate action—and such a thorough procedure may in turn discourage frivolous or ill-founded complaints.

Training should continue at every level of promotion, so that when an officer is promoted to a more responsible and complex job, he will not lose his bearings or mismanage his subordinates. Training in management and supervisory techniques, combined with ongoing psychiatric counseling, averts the kind of crisis that affected Dave Malkin's performance (see Chapter 7) and that inevitably weakens the performance of the entire department.

We can do many more things for our police. We can require the applicant to take two years of varied liberal arts courses (plus introductory police science) as a general student, then continue a concentrated curriculum in law enforcement for the next two years. This keeps him from becoming isolated from the people and issues he will deal with later.

In addition, the community should be encouraged to assist the police and to become better informed about their laws and rights. Citizen-police liaison committees will never work unless they include representatives from *all* sectors—

police, city council, business groups, private citizens, elected officials. These committees can do more than act as an intermediary between police and residents. They can develop new ideas for programs geared to specific community needs, such as a youth services bureau or alcohol or drug diversion programs; they can work with local social agencies to close the gap between police and the poor, homeless, unemployed, elderly, or ill; they can advise legislators about laws that are needed or that are not working at the community level; and they can research various options for screening applicants or providing in-service education for police. With all of this urgently needed work to be done in every city and community in the United States, it is disheartening to note that most police-citizen committees today are used as a public relations tool to whitewash activities of a bad cop or a bad department—or a bad citizen, for that matter, such as the prominent citizen arrested for drunk driving described in Chapter 10.

We can also help police by remembering that it is the psychological makeup of cops—not physical size, sex, or color—that determines the quality of their performance. Physical tests should reflect the actual work a police officer must do, not the prejudices of some cops or some community leaders who want to preserve the stereotyped "macho" image for police. Women, homosexuals, and members of minority races can of course be good cops if, like any other candidates, their personalities are stable and their motivation is to help, not punish, the people they serve.

The future of the good cop is inexorably tied to the future of our country as a free society. We can no longer neglect the needs of dedicated men and women whose job it is to preserve the American system of justice by serving *our* needs. If community leaders and police officials will not move to upgrade services to police through psychiatric in-service programs in all departments, then it is up to citizens themselves to demand it.

Appendix

The following discussion of psychological dynamics and the rescue fantasy motivation represents a composite of my lectures to police groups. This explanation is geared to the layman; thus, it covers basic points and does not attempt to encompass all of the complex medical terminology or theory in this area.

All forms of life share one primitive instinct—to preserve their own species through the cycle of reproduction. Each time a man and a woman engage in sex they are, on one level, responding to this primitive drive to fulfill their contract with nature to preserve the species.

Nature is a dynamic, forward-moving process. Therefore, the way man acts to preserve his species must be evaluated in relation to nature's drive for the preservation of life and the establishment of future generations. As man learns to use his sexual apparatus, he also develops certain attitudes toward his sexuality. The process of psychosexual identification can be understood only if one has a clear picture of the way man acts to oblige the instinct to preserve his species.

As man has become more civilized—perhaps technological is a better word—the establishment of sexual identity has become more difficult. Very early in his primitive development, he learned that inbreeding or incest was detrimental to the species and that crossbreeding or mongrelization was much healthier. This observation led to taboos against incest, which modern society still upholds. Yet the adoption of these taboos complicated the process of the child's personality development in its search for sexual identity.

Another factor in the complex mechanism of sexual identification is the length of the maturation process of the human species. For most animals, this process is relatively short and direct. Even primitive man matured in ten years, but the same process takes modern man twenty-five years. Although the increased length of the maturation process is more related to economics and education than to physiology, the extended period creates additional psychological complications for contemporary man.

NORMAL SEXUAL DEVELOPMENT

The development of sexual identity in a "normal" person might be described as an inverted triangle: in the top left corner, the female symbol—the mother—appears; opposite it is the male symbol; and at the bottom are the combined symbols of male and female, representing the child. One side of the triangle represents the male child's relationship with his mother; the second side represents his relationship with his father. The third side represents the father and mother's relationship, and completes the triangle of interactions. (A male child is discussed here because the majority of police are men; but this example of development also applies to the female child, with the parents in opposite roles.)

The infant begins life with two basic needs: to be fed and to be kept clean. Warmth is provided instinctively by the parent. Desires and feelings begin with birth and become more defined as the child grows and develops. At an early age, children find pleasure in touching their bodies. In so doing, they are awakening the early sexual drives that will be necessary for them to carry on the species. The developing direction of sexual interest of the infant is always toward the opposite sex—male to female, female to male. Any deviation from this scheme is considered an abnormality.

When the child begins to crawl, at six to ten months of age, he becomes aware of another need besides nourishment and cleanliness. At this time he experiences a strong desire to be closer to his mother and keep his father away. (And a female child experiences the same need to be closer to her father and to keep him away from her mother.)

However, his interests become thwarted from several sources. First, his parents set limits on his aggressive interest. And his own immature, undifferentiated sexual feelings may confuse as well as thwart him. For example, a young child may often confuse his mother's breasts and his father's penis. He must clarify many such examples of confusion to emerge into a clearly identified person.

The major foundations for sexual identification are developed in the child's first five or six years. As sexual identification proceeds, many other forces help forge the personality and point it in the direction of adult behavior, job interest, and general life goals. His desire to possess his mother and exclude his father is demonstrated in several ways, but the most common is the little boy's statement that he would like to marry his mother. When he is asked about his father, the boy's response is usually something vague: "Oh, he will go away." In effect, he states that he can take care of his mother, be a husband to her and father to himself. The orientation of this desire is sexual. But the boy is in a precarious position, and he realizes this when he notes his father's size and firm stand regarding his mother. He becomes unconsciously aware that he cannot be too aggressive in his demands for his mother's attention and decides on circumvention rather than frontal assault.

The process ideally moves further toward resolving the "What I am" image of maleness when the child begins to understand that to please both parents, he must try to be like his father. A firm, loving father will set a behavior pattern that his son can follow, and an understanding mother will reinforce it. The child in effect decides: "If I behave and act like my father, he will approve of me and be my friend. And if I treat my mother as he does, then my mother will not be able to tell us apart. She will let me take care of her and I will become her man." Thus, the child acquires his male identity and remains in harmony with his parents. His father is proud of the "chip off the old block," and his mother can speak of her "little man." This early process of evolution toward the establishment of the child's sexual identity is also known as the first Oedipal stage. It ends gradually and the child enters a less sexually active phase, one that tends to direct him to limit his play to his peer males.

Sometimes this second period, between ages six and twelve, is called the dormant or homosexual phase of development. It is the time when reinforcement of his male identification takes place. The boy does not like to be seen with girls. He seeks to excel and compete with other boys in sports and other activities, and his emotional ties at this time lie with his male peers. Sex play during this phase springs from curiosity in response to sexual desire; this phase is really a testing period for the child's identity of maleness.

The third phase of psychosexual identification is puberty. Male-female attraction awakens the triangle relations. Sexual identification is no longer an internal experience, but is now experienced in relation to the opposite sex and carries with it the possibility of completing the sex act for the creation of new life. Also known as the second Oedipal stage, this is a most unstable time for the individual. It is during this phase that the resolving of one's attachment to one's parents—the relationship of the triangle—becomes so important in determining the stability of one's adult life.

Any frustration at this point may lead to a volcanic response. The rebellion of the teenager becomes very important to him: if his parents' generation are clean-shaven, he wants a beard; if they have short hair, his is long; if they insist upon orderliness and cleanliness, his room is chaos and his grooming negligible. When he enters puberty the boy does so with a challenge based not on bravery, but on fear of confronting the adult. He uses the technique of challenge to cover up his own immaturity, often with little realization of why he is doing so. Many children at this age find their restrictions at home so imposing that they feel they must run away as a form of challenge or escape.

This turbulent period of sexual identification requires the most understanding from the parents—the most firmness, the most love and affection. For this is the first time that the child may act on his own, with consequences that can affect him for the rest of his life. And this is when the young person must resolve his own identity and his relationship with his parents. (And this is the period when most juvenile offenses are committed.)

The mechanism for resolving this triangle relationship depends on many factors, but ideally it is accomplished through mutual agreement between parents and child that the child must learn to take care of himself. He gradually gives up his infantile fantasy about usurping his father's place, instead of concentrating his attention on girls of his own age. When this state is finally behind, so usually are the "terrible teens." The child becomes a young adult, ready to take his place in society and to begin a new generation.

THE RESCUE FANTASY

During the first and third phases of personality development other forces may enter into the triangle, to form the personality that will seek its gratification in doing acts of service, in caring for people in trouble. This is one example of development that does not follow the ideal course. Under these circumstances growth and maturation take on less defined male or female identification, so that deviation or even reversal of roles takes place. The individual may show symptoms ranging from mild neurotic tendencies to severe psychotic behavior.

The basic motivation to help people begins in the first Oedipal phase, when the child is trying to usurp his father's place. Part of this instinct is to protect his mother from his father, especially if he has misinterpreted an act of intimacy he may have observed as an attack on his mother. The child also wants his mother for himself, and when he is stealing her away from his father, he is in effect rescuing her from his father, who possesses her. In the child's mind, stealing and rescue become the same thing, since it involves the child taking someone he feels belongs to him. To a limited extent, this rescue fantasy occurs in every child's development.

If the mother indicates that the father is mistreating her and the father behaves in a way that confirms this, the fantasy of the need to rescue his mother becomes a reality. But because of his size and inability to carry out the rescue, the child must suppress this fantasy. This urge to rescue enters the boy's unconscious, where it programs him to seek gratification by responding to this infantile memory. Whether in a positive or a negative way, he helps people in trouble; this satisfies his deep-seated need to rescue his mother.

The rescue fantasy has fascinated storytellers for centuries and can be seen as the theme in narratives from Sleeping Beauty to Popeye. The Saturday morning cartoons on television, for instance, can reinforce the child's fantasy about growing up to be a superadult or superhuman, able to perform real rescues. Persistence of a certain degree of need to rescue the mother from the father is necessary for a man to be able to feel the need to care for his own family.

In some persons the rescue fantasy finds an exaggerated or infantile expression. A fourteen- or fifteen-year-old boy or girl who shoots one parent for abusing the other is such an instance. I suspect that runaways have an unconscious wish to murder their neglecting parents and instead run from this urge to kill and at the same time try to punish their parents. Most people, however, find socially acceptable ways of venting their feelings of anger at a parent who is inadequate. They may move to another part of the country or break off contact with their parents to avoid a difficult situation.

Ideally, when the child reaches the end of the first Oedipal phase, the need to rescue his mother is realistically relegated to a minor role. In this case, the mother communicates that the father is doing an adequate job and the father's behavior confirms this. Thus, the child seeks other goals for his life work; nonhumanitarian jobs, skilled and unskilled.

POLICE AND THE RESCUE FANTASY

During my first interviews with policemen, I was surprised to discover that most officers gained their greatest satisfaction from police work when they felt that they had helped someone. This is, of course, a complete reversal of the familiar stereotype of a police officer as someone who is "out to get you." Another surprise was the high proportion of broken homes in these men's backgrounds. The circumstances of their childhoods might have included an alcoholic parent or parents, desertion by one or both parents, or a home virtually without parents because of the disabling aspects of addiction.

In the backgrounds of another large group of police were "covert" broken homes in which both parents were present. Often there would be no open arguments or problems, but the child just knew that his parents didn't get along. One or both parents were in such passive roles that for all practical purposes they didn't exist in the home.

Such a background seemed unlikely for the type of work that police do until I related it to the rescue fantasy. In a covert broken home, the rescue fantasy operates in such a way that the parent may be passive but communicates to the child (in exactly the same fashion as in the overt broken home) that the father is doing an inadequate job of caring for the family. His passiveness in itself communicates his inability to take care of the mother and child. Very often the child reacts to this passiveness with anger in order to provoke the father into some kind of open acceptance of his role. Because the parent rarely does accept this role, the rescue fantasy is established firmly, and the child's chance of openly resolving his anger at the passive parent is almost nil. The child from an overt broken home has a better chance of resolving his feelings about his parents because there is an open conflict he can relate to and decide how to deal with.

It is important to understand that the original resolution of the triangle relationships will determine the demeanor of the individual as he helps others. If the individual is sublimated and the fantasy is part of the ego structure of self-satisfaction, he will show kindness and reasonable, sensible behavior. The reactive person will tend toward overresponse, harshness, and "rescues" involving the use of brute force.

The sublimated person has integrated this fantasy as part of his ego structure of self-satisfaction. The reactive person is characterized by nonintegration of this fantasy; it is used by the superego to ward off the opposing desire to wreak havoc on the individual's ego. The sublimated person is a good police candidate; the reactive person is not. Under stress, the reactive person's superego controls may give way and his angry, destructive feelings may surface. The result is the brutal fury that has been seen all too often in police behavior.

Persons in whom the rescue fantasy is strong have certain other characteristics, such as the need to be alert to anyone who might become an aggressor toward the parent to be rescued—hence the high index among police for being suspicious or paranoid. Another characteristic is group loyalty, which stems from the need to prove one's loyalty to the parent to be rescued. The aggressive reaction also is part of the complex—a desire to take aggressive, decisive action to stop a threatening force from attacking.

All of this subtle interaction of forces within the mind underlines the particular difficulties of choosing the right men and women for the police. It is not possible to deal with the problems of police, let alone solve them, unless the rescue fantasy is understood and used as a basis for working with the special type of people we must attract to and train for police work.

Bibliography and Reader's Guide

Abraham, Karl. "The Rescue and Murder of the Father in Neurotic Fantasy Formation." *Clinical Papers and Essays on Psychoanalytics,* Chapter XV. London, 1955.

A detailed, technical study of the rescue fantasy, but without special reference to police or law enforcement.

Bainbridge, J. "Profiles—Constable." *New Yorker,* 14 August 1971, pp. 40–53.

This profile of the British bobby illustrates the universality of police: their backgrounds, training, responses, and attitudes.

Banton, Michael. *Policeman in the Community.* New York: Basic Books, 1965.

A meticulous comparison of an American police department to an English police department. This anthropological study of the two departments and their communities is probably the best available on police attitudes and behavior.

Bennett-Sandler, Georgette, and Ubell, Earl. "Time Bombs in Blue." *New York Magazine,* 3 March 1976, pp. 47ff.

Bordua, David J., ed. *Police: Six Sociological Essays.* New York: Wiley, 1967.

A review of the concept of law and order.

Buckley, Tom. "Murphy Among the 'Meat-Eaters.'" *New York Times Magazine*, 19 December 1971, pp. 8ff.

A report on Police Commissioner Patrick V. Murphy and his fight to clear the New York City Police Department of "meat-eaters"—policemen who actively seek payoffs.

Cain, Maureen E. *Society and the Policeman's Role*. Boston: Routledge & Kegan, 1973.

A good reference on the role of the beat patrol officer and the service aspect of his or her job.

Campbell, James S.; Sahid, Joseph R.; and Stang, David P. *Law and Order Reconsidered: Report of the Task Force on Law and Law Enforcement to the National Commission on the Causes and Prevention of Violence*. New York: Bantam Books, 1970.

An in-depth analysis of legal, social, and political institutions. This is not a report of the Commission itself.

Challenge of Crime in a Free Society. Report of the President's Commission on Law Enforcement and Administration of Justice. Washington, D.C.: U.S. Government Printing Office, 1967.

Clark, Ramsey. *Crime in America*. New York: Simon and Schuster, 1970.

A consideration of the nature, cause and prevention of crime by former U. S. Attorney General Clark. He discusses the limitations of police ability and the paradox that crime statistics rise when police efficiency increases.

Critchley, T.A. *History of Police in England and Wales 900–1966*. London: Constable, 1966.

Excellent historical review of law enforcement from the Frankpledge period of the post-Roman Empire to modern times. Includes the full text of Peel's Metropolitan Act of 1829. The detailed bibliography includes both source material and a chronology.

Critchley, T.A. *History of Police in England and Wales*. 2nd rev. ed. Montclair, N.J.: Patterson, Smith, 1973.

Some added and more up-to-date material. The first edition of this book contains more detailed information on early police.

Freud, Sigmund. *The Complete Psychological Works of Sigmund Freud*.

London: Hogarth Press and Institute of Psychoanalysis, 1957–1958. Volumes V, VI, and XI.

Here Freud lays the groundwork of the rescue fantasy theory, its motivations and use in dream interpretation. My "triangle of life" theory owes much to Freud's discussion in Volumes VI and XI.

Germann, A.C., et. al. *Introduction to Law Enforcement and Criminal Justice.* Springfield, Illinois: C.C. Thomas, 1976.

A general history with a discussion of law enforcement in the Babylonian, Iranian and Egyptian periods; it also touches on the Chinese contribution.

Hopkins, Ernest J. *Our Lawless Police.* New York: Da Capo Press, 1972.

Kifner, John. "Men in the Middle." *New York Times Magazine,* 12 September 1976, pp. 36ff.

The story of the police officers of Boston caught between "their roots and law and order" during the stormy school busing debate.

Kreins, E.; Cain, T.; Nunnes, J.; Harn, K.; Shev, Edward E., M.D. "Youth Service Bureau Final Report." Pleasant Hill Police Department, Pleasant Hill, California, 1971–1974.

Outlines a system of diverting juvenile offenders from the juvenile court system by involving parents and community.

Kreins, Edward S., and Shev, Edward E., M.D. "Psychiatric Techniques in the Selection and Training of Police Officers." *The Police Chief,* April 1968, pp. 10–13.

"Law and Order," *Time,* 4 October 1968.

Levy, Burton. "Cops in the Ghetto." *American Behavioral Scientist,* March 1968, pp. 31–34.

National Advisory Commission on Civil Disorders. New York: Bantam, 1968.

Perlstein, Gary R. "Policewomen and Policemen." *The Police Chief,* 3 March 1972, pp. 72–83.

An analysis of the performances of men and women as police officers. The study suggests the two sexes have equal professional capabilities.

Pound, Roscoe. *Criminal Justice in America*. New York: Da Capo Press, 1972.

A history which confirms the idea that police problems are universal and continuous.

Preiss, Jack J., and Ehrlich, Howard J. *Examination of Role Theory: The Case of the State Police*. Lincoln, Nebraska: University of Nebraska Press, 1966.

Defines the position of the police officer in a free society, and the ways in which officers use discretionary authority.

Reiss, Albert J., Jr. *The Police and the Public*. New Haven, Connecticut: Yale University Press, 1973.

Study of corruption among police by Yale's Institute for Social and Policy Studies.

A Report on the San Francisco Police Department. San Francisco: Western Star Press, 1971.

Schlossberg, Harvey, and Freeman, Lucy. *Psychologist with a Gun*. New York: Coward, McCann and Geoghegan, Inc., 1974.

The author is a sergeant and a resident psychologist in the New York City Police Department. He describes his program of identifying and counseling disturbed cops, and educating all police officers in violence, mental illness, etc.

Shev, Edward E., M.D., and Wright, James. "The Uses of Psychiatric Techniques in Selecting and Training Police Officers as Part of Their Regular Training." *Police*, May–June, 1971, pp. 13–16.

Skolnick, Jerome. *Politics of Protest*. New York: Ballantine Books, 1969.

Veysey, Laurence, ed. *Law and Resistance: American Attitudes Toward Authority*. New York: Harper and Row, 1970.

An analysis of American patterns of thinking and behavior in respect to lawlessness, with one section devoted to the role of police in America.

°Wilson, Orlando W. *Police Planning*, 2nd ed. Springfield, Illinois: C.C. Thomas, 1973.

°Wilson, Orlando W., and McCaren, Roy C. *Police Administration*. 3rd ed. New York: McGraw-Hill, 1972.

°These two volumes are used by almost all police academies and police departments in the education of police officers.

Index

210

212

213

EDWARD E. SHEV, M.D. was born in 1919 in Lincoln, Nebraska, and completed his residency in neurology at the University of California School of Medicine in 1951. He has been president of both the National Association of the Visually Handicapped and the Western Electroencephalography Society, and is a frequent contributor to medical journals on such subjects as syphillis, aging, epilepsy, heart disease, herpes simplex, tranquilizers, and many other subjects. Today he maintains his private practice in San Francisco and is also Chief of Neurology at the Marshal Hale Memorial Hospital in that city. He lives with his wife and daughter in Sausalito.

JEREMY JOAN HEWES is the author of *Build Your Own Playground!* and Senior Editor of the *California Management Review* at the School of Business Administration at the University of California, Berkeley.